The Days of the Prophets

What We Can Learn From Biblical Prophecy

To John & Nan

David Teeter

David Teeter

Outskirts Press, Inc.
Denver, Colorado

CONTENTS

PREFACE

Many people have told me they find the biblical prophets too confusing or disturbing. So these inspired passages are often skipped over. I am always saddened to see the prophetic scriptures misapplied or ignored. I hope that this book will help clear away some of this confusion and apprehension.

The Days of the Prophets is a product of my life-long love of the Bible as a Bible teacher, scholar, and pastor. About half of my working life has been teaching Bible in Christian colleges.

My previous book on prophetic scripture, *The Kingdom Suffers Violence*, 1975, is now out of print. I considered having it republished. But thirty some years have elapsed since I wrote that book.

Those years included eleven years (1978-1989) in the Holy Land, teaching at Bethlehem Bible College, and directing an off-campus Friendship Center for Muslim university students.

In Jerusalem, I was able to interact with biblical scholars from around the world. I also studied Judaism under Jewish teachers at Hebrew University's Martin Buber Institute while doing two years of doctoral research on the three religions of the Holy Land.

These experiences have enriched my own Christian faith as well as giving me some fresh perspectives on the prophetic scriptures.

Living in Bethlehem, my wife and I were caught in the middle of the Israeli-Palestinian conflict. We saw firsthand how misguided ideas of biblical prophecy have inflamed ethnic rivalries in the "Land of Promise."

The Days of the Prophets is certainly not the final and complete answer to the difficult passages of biblical prophecy. But the insights I am sharing have made a difference in my life, and hopefully, you will find them insightful and helpful as well.

INTRODUCTION

I was eleven years old in 1948, when the State of Israel was born. I was excited because our pastor told us that Israel was God's signpost for the return of Christ. He told us that all prophecies leading up to the Rapture were now fulfilled. He fully expected the Rapture to occur before the end of the year.

As Christmas drew near, I worried about my presents, which I knew were hidden in the hall closet. What if the Rapture came before Christmas, and I never got to open my presents? If that happened, might I at least know, up in heaven, what my presents were?

Needless to say, Christmas morning arrived on schedule, and I got to open my presents.

Growing up in church, I heard countless sermons on the imminent Rapture. We were warned that back-slidden or lukewarm Christians probably would not go up in the rapture. Missing the Rapture meant facing the Antichrist in the seven year Great Tribulation.

Evangelists came to our church with prophecy charts. These charts claimed to show the events that would lead to the rapture, and the role of today's nations in these events. But in all this Second Coming preaching, the actual message of the prophets somehow got "left behind."

I had nightmares about the Rapture happening. In these dreams I would strain to rise, but was never able to get off the ground.

This was my childhood experience with Bible prophecy.

Some years later, I discovered that my childhood teachings were based on a system of theology called "Dispensationalism." This system was developed in the 1830's by the Irish-Anglo preacher Charles Nelson Darby.

Darby's system splits Christ's return into two events: First, a secret Rapture, in which believing Christians would be caught up to heaven. Seven years later, Christ would make his public return from heaven. In between these two events would be a seven year Great Tribulation, with the world dominated by the Antichrist.

(There are variations of this End Time scenario. Some believe the Rapture will occur midway through the Great Tribulation. A few believe that the Rapture will occur at the end of the tribulation.)

Another feature of Darby's system is his treatment of Israel. Darby believed that God has two chosen peoples, Israel and the Church. During the millennium, Israel will be on earth and the Church will be in heaven. The return of the Jewish people to the promised land would signal that the rapture of the church was imminent. Christian Zionism springs from these roots.

End Time scenarios derived from Darby's system usually reflect the following assumptions about biblical prophecy:

- **Futuristic**—Bible prophecies are mostly about still future events, and especially events surrounding the Second Coming.

- **Deterministic**—current and future events are pre-determined by biblical prophecy.
- **Literal-nationalistic**—God's promise to Abraham and his descendents must be fulfilled in a literal State of Israel before the Second Coming. The temple will be rebuilt and sacrifices resumed.
- **Pre-millennial**—Christ's return takes place before the Millennium. Christ's millennial reign takes place on earth. (See Robert Clouse for an excellent discussion on four views of the Millennium.) (Clouse 1977)

I believe these ideas are based on faulty interpretation of scripture. Darby's sequence of Rapture-Tribulation-Return of Christ is nowhere set forth in scripture. Supporters of this approach take scattered verses from their biblical-historical setting and plug them into Darby's scenario as "proof texts."

Nevertheless, Darby's system spread to America in the early 1900's. A Dr. Cyrus Scofield wrote a Dispensational commentary, which he worked into the Bible in footnotes. This became the famous *Scofield Bible*.

Generations of Christians grew up knowing only the *Scofield Bible*. (My first Bible was a children's *Pilgrim's Edition* of the *Scofield Bible*.) As a result, Darby's Rapture-Tribulation-Second Coming scenario was widely adopted by fundamentalist groups in America.

More recently, Darby's End Time system has been popularized in such books as Lindsey's *Late Great Planet Earth* series, LaHaye's *Left Behind* series, and numerous other books, movies, and sermons.

Gary DeMar does a good job of biblically refuting

these "end time" assumptions in his book, *End Time Fiction.* (DeMar 2001).

My approach, however, is to focus on the message of the prophets that so often is ignored in all the controversies over the "End Time."

The prophets of the Bible cannot give you tomorrow's headlines. But they do have a message which speaks to every age, including ours. My purpose in writing *Days of the Prophets* is to make this message more easily accessible.

The Days of the Prophets is not a book by book or verse by verse commentary. I don't have an explanation for every detail or vision. There are good commentaries that can help with verse by verse studies. I have included some in my bibliography.

Instead, each chapter of *Days of the Prophets* highlights one important theme of biblical prophecy. We begin with the Hebrew prophets of the Old Testament. We continue with the prophetic words of Jesus, and conclude with the book of Revelation.

I hope as you read this book you will find insights and ideas that will help you:

- Be better able to discern the hand of God in the times in which we live.
- Live more confidently and faithfully through dark and difficult times.
- Live in the hope that sustained the biblical prophets and can sustain us as well.
- Have a fresh vision of God's redemptive purposes for this world and for these times.

CHAPTER 1

The World of the Prophets
Whose Future Did the Prophets Foresee?

When times are good, be happy; but when times are bad, consider: God has made the one as well as the other. Therefore a man cannot discover anything about his future. (Eccl 7:14)

Each day has enough troubles of its own. (Matt. 6:34)

God raised up the biblical prophets to speak to their nation in times of crisis. These prophets were not concerned about events of our time 2600 years in their future. Nor were they concerned about today's China, America, Russia, or Germany. They had troubles enough in their own day, with their own nation poised on the brink of disaster.

To understand the message of the prophets, we need to put ourselves back in their world, see their concerns and issues, and observe how and when their prophesies were fulfilled in history. That is our task in this chapter.

By "biblical prophets," I mean the prophets whose messages make up the major and minor prophetic books of the Old Testament, Isaiah through Malachi. These prophets lived during three periods of national crisis:

The Assyrian crisis which brought an end to the

Kingdom of Israel. This crisis era began about 740 BC, and concluded with the destruction of Samaria in 721 BC.[1]

The Babylonian crisis which brought an end to the Kingdom of Judah. This crisis began in 609 BC, and concluded with the destruction of Jerusalem, in 586 BC.

The post-exilic period, when Jews were returning to Jerusalem to rebuilding their national life, from 538 to about 400 BC.

After Solomon's death, around 960 BC, the Kingdom of Israel was split into two kingdoms. The northern tribes kept the name **Israel**. The capital of Israel was Samaria, some 60 miles north of Jerusalem.

The southern tribes became the Kingdom of **Judah**. It's capital was Jerusalem, where the temple built by Solomon was located.

The prophets of the northern kingdom of Israel were **Hosea, Amos and Jonah.** These men all prophesied during the reign of the same king, Jeroboam II (793-753). He was a strong and effective ruler, but not a godly one.

He did evil in the eyes of the Lord and did not turn away from any of the sins of Jeroboam, son of Nebat, which he had caused Israel to commit. (2 Kings 14: 24)

The *sins of Jeroboam* refers to the golden calf shrines the first Jeroboam built at the northern and southern borders of Israel. The purpose of these shrines was to sever religious ties with the temple in Jerusalem. This policy was continued by all the kings of Israel, including Jeroboam II. (1 Kings 12:25)

In spite of Jeroboam's state-sponsored idolatry, God had pity on the people of Israel and gave them a period of calm, stability, and prosperity under Jeroboam II.

The Lord had seen how bitterly everyone in Israel, whether slave or free, was suffering; there was no one to help them. And since the Lord had not said he would blot out the name of Israel from under heaven, he saved them by the hand of Jeroboam, son of Joash. (2 Kings 14:27)

God had promised Jeroboam's great-grandfather Jehu that he and his descendents would rule over Israel for four generations. Jeroboam II was the fourth generation. He was the end of the line of Jehu's family.

The prophets understood that this was Israel's last chance to avert national disaster. They were appalled at not only the state-sponsored idolatry, but about the oppression of the poor and powerless at that hands of the rich and powerful. Each of the prophets had a different way of telling their story:

Hosea was told by the Lord to marry a prostitute. His frustrations with her continued infidelities became a parable of God's frustrations with Israel's continuing idolatry.

With their silver and gold they make idols for themselves to their own destruction. Throw out your calf-idol, O Samaria! This calf— a craftsman has made it; it is not God. It will be broken in pieces, that calf of Samaria. (Hos. 8:5,6)

Amos was a poor itinerate farm worker from east of Bethlehem. God sent him to Bethel, the border town between Israel and Judah. He preached against the Bethel shrine with its golden calf, and the injustices of the wealthy ruling class:

For I know how many are your offences and how great your sins. You oppress the righteous and take bribes, and you deprive the poor of justice in your courts. Therefore the prudent man keeps quiet in such times, for the times are evil. (Amos 5: 12,13)

Jonah was a supporter of Jeroboam II and a fierce patriot. Jonah's support was a major factor in Jeroboam's success. But one day God told Jonah to go to Nineveh, the Assyrian capital, and preach to the Assyrians.

Jonah didn't want to go. He saw the Assyrians as the "evil empire" and was eager for God's judgment to fall upon them. But God had his way and Jonah went. To his great chagrin, the Assyrians repented, and God spared Nineveh. But Jonah's mission succeeded in giving Israel a time of peace under Jeroboam II.

Jonah teaches us a valuable lesson: Our enemies are not always God's enemies. God may be working on our enemies in ways unknown to us.

All three of these prophets had the same concern: Time was running out for Israel. The king and the people were blindly going down the road to disaster. The disaster they all foresaw would come at the hands of the Assyrians.

THE ASSYRIAN CRISIS

Israel's grace period ended with the death of Jeroboam in 753 BC. What followed was a 26 year period of instability and decline. A series of weak kings followed who continued to *do evil in the sight of the Lord.* **Hosea** continued to prophesy during this period.

The crisis began with the Assyrian invasion of the Galilee in 727 BC. The Galilean tribes were taken away into captivity. The Assyrians then returned and lay siege to Samaria, the capital of Israel. In 721 BC, the city was conquered and destroyed, its people taken away and scattered to the four winds. That was the end of the kingdom of Israel.

The Assyrians followed up their victory over Israel with an invasion of Judah. But Judah had the benefit of godly king Hezekiah and the prophets **Isaiah** and **Micah.** Isaiah encouraged Hezekiah to stand fast, and the Assyrian invasion was turned back. So Judah's final crisis was postponed for a century.

The prophets of **Judah** were **Nahum, Zephaniah, Habakkuk, Micah,** and **Jeremiah.** Except for **Micah,** these all prophesied during the reign of the same king, the godly young King Josiah (640-609 BC). Micah was a contemporary of Isaiah, a century earlier than Jeremiah and the others.

The young king instituted a series of dramatic reforms. He ordered the destruction of pagan idols throughout the land. He sponsored a major refurbishment of the temple. He sponsored the greatest Passover celebration in many decades.

Nahum's prophecy was directed against the Assyrians, who soon came into judgment at the hands of the Babylonians.

Zephaniah prophesied about God's coming judgment against Judah's neighboring kingdoms, and against the Assyrians. But his sharpest criticism was directed against his own Jerusalem and Judah.

5

Habakkuk warned about the surging Babylonians, who would precipitate the coming crisis.

Jeremiah foresaw an invasion coming from the north. Later, when the Babylonians defeated the Assyrians at Carchemish in 605 BC, Jeremiah recognized the Babylonians as the danger.

These prophets generally supported the reforms of King Josiah, but were concerned that the reforms were not penetrating to the hearts of the people.

Then came disaster. King Josiah was killed in battle in 609 BC, at age 39. This tragedy will be discussed further in the chapter on Armageddon.

Josiah's death precipitated a crisis for the kingdom of Judah. Josiah's sons made a series of bad decisions. Against the advice of Jeremiah, they tried to play off the Egyptians against the surging Babylonians. This folly set the stage for the final disaster.

Jeremiah urged the kings of Judah to submit to the yoke of Babylon. King Jehoiakim first complied, and then, against Jeremiah's advice, rebelled. Jehoiakim died in 597 BC, and was succeeded by the 18 year old Jehoiachin. He lasted three months.

The final crisis began in 597 BC, when young King Jehoiachin was taken hostage to Babylon. **Ezekiel** and **Daniel** were also taken. Josiah's uncle Zedekiah was installed as king in his place. Zedekiah respected Jeremiah and protected him, but rejected his advice.

Jeremiah wrote letters to the Jews in exile. His letters gave Ezekiel and Daniel guidance. He told them that the Babylon empire would last for 70 years. He gave the Jewish exiles a strategy for survival, and the hope that their descendants would one day return to the land of promise.

6

The end came in 586 BC, when Jerusalem fell to the Babylonian army. The city was burned, the temple destroyed, and the survivors taken to Babylon. This brought to a bitter end the kingdom of Judah established by King David 400 years earlier.

Obadiah prophesied against the Edomites for their mistreatment of Jews fleeing from the Babylonians.

The biblical prophets continued their work during the exile. **Ezekiel** gave the Jews in exile a vision of a restored nation. Disciples of **Isaiah** continued to prophesy in Isaiah's name and spirit. Isaiah chapters 40 through 55 were probably written during this period.

THE RETURN TO ZION (539-400 BC)

After the Persian conquest of Babylon in 539 BC, Jews were granted permission to return to Jerusalem to rebuild the temple. This story is told in Ezra and Nehemiah.

The prophets of this period were **Haggai**, **Zechariah**, **Joel**, and **Malachi**.

The first group of returning Jews built an altar and laid the foundation of the temple. But conflict with the Samaritans resulted in a Persian stop work order. The temple project was abandoned for seventeen years.

Then **Haggai** and **Zechariah** began to prophesy. They encouraged the people to resume the temple project. Permission was obtained, and the temple was completed in 521 BC. **Isaiah** chapters 56-66 may also belong to this period.

Almost a century passed before the story picks up again in the book of Ezra. There were some hard times, an extended economic depression. Many of the Jews abandoned Jerusalem and returned to their ancestral villages to survive by farming.

The book of Joel probably belongs to this period. Joel reports an extended drought followed by a locust plague.

The story picks up around 440 BC with the arrival of Ezra with a new edition of the Law of Moses. The prophet **Malachi** belongs to this period. Many scholars believe that the books of **Ruth** and **Jonah** were written during this time, perhaps as a prophetic protest against the anti-foreign emphasis of Ezra and Nehemiah.

These were the days of the biblical prophets. According to Jewish tradition, the spirit of prophecy was lifted after Malachi, around 400 BC.

THE ROLE OF THE PROPHET

There were three anointed offices that made up the government of ancient Israel - the priesthood, the king, and the prophets.

The priests were a conservative force in ancient Israel. In addition to their sacramental duties, they were teachers of the law, served as health inspectors, and settled domestic disputes.

The priesthood was an inherited office. They were anointed with oil as a symbol of their spiritual qualifications for office. In Judah, they usually supported the throne.

The kings represented the executive office in Israel and Judah. The king was usually anointed with oil by the prophet and/or the priest as the symbol of his spiritual qualities.

In the northern kingdom of Israel, "regime change" often came by assassination. The longest dynasty lasted just four generations. All the kings of the northern kingdom were said to *do evil in the sight of the Lord.*

In Judah, the dynasty of David ruled throughout. Some kings were good; some evil; some good in their early years before turning evil in their latter years. The more godly kings supported the priesthood, and the priesthood supported the king.

The prophet represented the independent branch of the governments of Israel and Judah, somewhat like our news media. The prophet did not depend on priests or kings for their anointing. They received their anointing directly from the Holy Spirit. Inspired preaching was their badge of office.

Some of the biblical prophets were influential members of their community. They had the ear of the king. Isaiah served as King Uzziah's court historian and was probably a cousin of the king.

Others were from a priestly background, as were Jeremiah and Ezekiel. Others were outside the center of political power, but held in high esteem by the common people, such as Hosea, Amos, and Micah.

It was their job to speak "inconvenient truth" to power. It was often their lot to tell the king what he didn't want to hear. No life insurance company would have wanted these prophets as clients.

In the Middle East, and even in Israel, many kings hired professional "prophets." Their job was to extol the king's virtues and whip up the courage of the army by prophecies of glorious victory. In other words, they served as cheerleaders for the king's military adventures.

In Solomon's kingdom, court prophets were drawn from the ranks of the priests and Levites. Along with the musicians, they were members of the royal choir. Apparently, this practice continued with the kings of Judah. (See 2 Chron. 25)

The biblical prophets were often opposed by the official court prophets. You can read of Jeremiah's conflict with some of these "court prophets" in Jeremiah chapters 26 and 28.

THE MESSAGE OF THE PROPHETS

In general, we could sum up the prophet's message as follows:

- They addressed the personal sins of the people, such as theft, murder, immorality, and idolatry. But the greater judgment was directed at national sins. They condemned the oppression of the poor and powerless by the rich and powerful.
- They warned that the kingdom had entered a critical era. The present course would only lead to disaster. This disaster could be averted, but only by profound national repentance. Superficial religious activity would not suffice.
- They offered hope to the faithful remnant that God had not forsaken His people. What seemed to be the end of everything would prove to be a new beginning.

Usually, the prophet's warnings went unheeded. The people could not believe that God was no longer on their side. After all, they were God's chosen people.

Disaster came as prophesied, usually in the form of an invading army. The prophets regarded the invader as an instrument of God's judgment upon a faithless and disobedient nation.

But the message of the prophets was not all judgmental. They offered inspiring visions of God's purpose in Israel. Isaiah and Micah's vision of a redeemed Zion, with the nations coming to learn the ways of the Lord, is one of the most inspiring visions in scripture. (Isa. 2 and Micah 4)

Another inspiring vision of Isaiah is the subject of my chapter 3, **A Highway To Assyria**.

THE PROPHETIC HORIZON

How far into the future were the prophets able to see? Hosea, Amos, and Micah prophesied between 760 and 740 BC. The judgments they prophesied came to pass in 721 BC.

In the southern kingdom of Judah, the prophets Nahum, Zephaniah, Habakkuk, and Jeremiah began their work early in the reign of king Josiah, around 640 BC. The disaster they foresaw came to pass in 586 BC with the fall of Jerusalem.

From biblical history we can see that their prophetic horizon extended into the future for one or two generations, or some 20 to 40 years.

The prophets did have brief glimpses of a future beyond this horizon. They sensed in the Spirit that their prophecies had a deeper meaning beyond the issues of their day. There were glimpses of a coming redeemer-messiah, as Peter explained much later:

The prophets searched intently and with great care, trying to find out the time and circumstances to which the Spirit of Christ in them was pointing, when he predicted the sufferings of Christ, and the glories that would follow. (1 Pet.1:11)

There were a few other exceptions. Isaiah's prophecy of the fall of Babylon was fulfilled 160 years later (if written by the original Isaiah). Jeremiah prophesied that the Jewish exile would last 70 years. The reason for these exceptions will be discussed in the next chapter, **Lessons in Pottery Making**.

The prophets were not able to look 2600 years into their future to predict events of our time. They had only fleeting glimpses of Christ's first coming, let alone Christ's Second Coming thousands of years in their future. They, like us, walked by faith.

We cannot look to the biblical prophets for tomorrow's headlines. Yet they do have a message that speaks to our day. We will explore different themes of that message in the chapters that follow.

But for the most part, the distant future remained hidden in "clouds of unknowing." What we can and cannot know will be discussed in the final chapter of this book.

Meanwhile, let's look briefly at the poetic imagery used by the prophets, and the nature of prophetic inspiration and interpretation.

PROPHETIC IMAGERY AND INSPIRATION

Scripture tells us, and I believe, that the prophets were inspired by the Holy Spirit. *Men spoke from God as they were carried along by the Holy Spirit.* (2 Pet.1:21)

But the Spirit's inspiration is not mechanical. God doesn't plug a word processor into the prophet's brain and download the message.

The Spirit worked within the prophet's own world view, literary style, emotions, intellect, and life experiences. The Spirit also worked through the prophet's imagination, intuition, and subconscious mind. Some prophets, like Ezekiel, found meaning in dreams and visions.

Set afire by the Spirit, they preached with passion and conviction. They often used vivid poetic imagery to stir the hearts of the people. For example:

See, the day of the Lord is coming—
a cruel day, with wrath and fierce anger—
To make the land desolate
and destroy the sinners within it.
The stars of heaven and their constellations
will not show their light.
The rising sun will be darkened
and the moon not give its light. (Isa.13: 9,10)

These poetic sermons were usually written down by the prophet's disciples. In some cases, schools founded by the prophet continued his work long after his death. They wrote in the prophet's name and spirit. Isaiah chapters 40-66 may have been produced in this manner.

Regardless of who actually penned the words, *All scripture is God-breathed.* (2 Tim.3:16)

I believe the same Holy Spirit who inspired the prophets is present with us today, to help us make sense of God's world, enlighten us to God's purposes, and open our eyes to the message of His ancient prophets.

CHAPTER 2

A Lesson in Pottery Making

The future is open; make the most of it.

Do not pray for this people nor offer any plea or petition for them, because I will not listen when they call to me in the time of their distress... Even if Moses and Samuel were to stand before me, my heart would not go out to this people. (Jer.11:14;15:1)

What if God stopped hearing our prayers? What hope would we have then? The prophet Jeremiah was faced with this very question, for this is what God was saying to him.

Jeremiah had begun his prophetic career in a time of national renewal and revival, led by the godly young King Josiah. It seemed that Judah was finally emerging from the dark decades of the rule of Josiah's grandfather, the wicked Manasseh.

But those hopes were violently dashed by King Josiah's untimely death in an unnecessary war.

2 Kings gives us this assessment of the situation upon the death of King Josiah:

The Lord did not turn away from the heat of his fierce anger, which burned against Judah because of all that Manasseh had done to provoke him to anger.

So the Lord said, "I will remove Judah also from my presence, as I removed Israel, and I will reject Je-

rusalem, the city I chose, and this temple, about which I said, 'There shall my Name be.'" (2 Kings 23:26)

If that was not bad enough, now the Lord orders Jeremiah to stop his prayers for Jerusalem.

For years, Jeremiah had been prophesying that God's judgment was coming upon Judah and Jerusalem. But he had always hoped for a reprieve. Now the situation looked hopeless, for the Lord told Jeremiah: *I have withdrawn my blessing, my love and my pity from this people, declares the Lord* (Jer.16:6)

Was there no hope? Had Jeremiah's prophecies of doom sealed the fate of Jerusalem? It must have seemed that way to Jeremiah.

At the Lord's direction, Jeremiah paid a visit to the house of the pottery maker. He watched as the potter removed a flawed pot from the wheel. The potter kneaded the pot back to a wet lump of clay. He put the clay back on the wheel and started over.

Watching the potter work with the clay, Jeremiah received a word from the Lord:

O house of Israel, can I not do with you as this potter does, declares the Lord. Like clay in the hand of the potter, so are you in my hand, O house of Israel.

Jeremiah realized that prophecy does not limit God's sovereignty. God is free to do as He wills. The Word continued:

If at any time I announce that a nation or kingdom is to be uprooted, torn down and destroyed, and if that nation I warned repents of its evil, then I will relent and not inflict on it the disaster I had planned. (Jer. 18:7-8)

In other words, **prophecies of judgment can be averted by repentance**.

There is a rabbinical saying: "the door of prayer is sometimes open, sometimes closed. But the door of repentance is ever open." (Cohen 1975)

Jeremiah was told that the door of prayer was closed. But the door of repentance was still open: Jeremiah told the people:

If you really **change your ways** *and your* **actions**, *and deal with each other justly, if you do not oppress the alien, the fatherless, or the widow and do not shed innocent blood in this place, and if you do not follow other gods to your own harm, then I will* **let you live in this place**, *in the land that I gave your forefathers forever and ever.* (Jer. 7:5-7)

But we cannot just take God's blessings for granted. The next verse gives us the other side of the coin:

And if at another time I announce that a nation or kingdom is to be built up and planted, and if it does evil in my sight and does not obey me, then I will reconsider the good I had intended to do for it. (Jer. 7:9,10)

So we see that prophecies of judgment can be averted by repentance, and promised blessings can be forfeited by unbelief and disobedience.

In Israel, someone showed me a newsletter they had received. The writer said: "To understand today's events, we must understand the prophecies that determine them... Prophecy is history pre-written."

That statement is just plain wrong. Today's events are not determined by biblical prophecy. The future is not pre-determined. Decisions being made now and in the future will determine our outcome.

Nothing is inevitable; nothing is impossible. Sure, a bloody Armageddon is still possible. As is national disintegration and collapse. Or a nuclear winter. But it doesn't have to happen.

We have an **open future**, full of possibilities, some good, and some bad. Biblical prophecy can make a difference if we will hear it out and embrace its insights.

The inspired Word can help us see how we have gone astray, what lies at the end of the path we are on, and what must be done to avert disaster. It is **our response** to that Word that will determine the outcome.

But suppose the people of Jerusalem in Jeremiah's day had fully repented. And suppose Jeremiah's prophecies of judgment never came to pass. Would Jeremiah be considered a false prophet if the judgment he prophesied never happened?

Not at all! God's purpose is to convince the people to turn back to God and change their ways. The prophecy is *fulfilled* if it accomplishes this purpose. God is sovereign; he is not bound to carry out the judgment once the prophecy's purpose has been achieved.

Even partial or temporary repentance can defer or moderate the prophesied judgment. For God *is patient, not wanting anyone to perish, but to come to repentance.* (2 Pet. 3:9)

There are good examples in scripture of judgment averted or amended by repentance.

Nineveh. Jonah prophesied *yet forty days and God will destroy Nineveh.* Nineveh was the capital of Assyria, the "evil empire" of Jonah's day. But the king and the people repented. Nineveh's day of doom was postponed for a century, much to Jonah's chagrin.

Judah and Jerusalem. The Assyrians invaded Judah in 715 BC, and threatened to destroy Jerusalem. But in Judah, the spiritual revival of King Hezekiah made the difference. With Isaiah's support, Hezekiah stood firm and the Assyrian invasion was repelled. Judah's repentance under King Hezekiah deferred its judgment for a century.

Babylon represents another example of prophecy deferred by repentance. Both Isaiah and Jeremiah prophesied in lurid apocalyptic imagery the destruction of Babylon. (See Isaiah 13 and Jeremiah 30)

An oracle concerning Babylon... See, the day of the Lord is coming - a cruel day, with wrath and fierce anger. To make the land desolate and destroy the sinners in it. The stars of heaven and their constellations will not show their light. The rising sun will be darkened... (Isa. 13:1,9ff)

But it never happened this way. For in Daniel, we read that King Nebuchadnezzar repented of his pride and arrogance. He humbled himself before the God of Israel. (Dan 4:28-37)

The Jews in exile were treated humanely, and some rose to high administrative posts. Babylon became a place of refuge for Jews during their exile, and a center of Jewish scholarship for many centuries to come.

Babylon was captured by the Persians in 539 BC. But the city was not destroyed. There was a regime change, but Babylon merely became a provincial capital of the Persian empire. Babylon lived on for another thousand years through many such regime changes.

We also have examples of blessings forfeited by disobedience. For example, God had promised King David:

I will provide a place for my people Israel and will plant them so that they can have a home of their own and no longer be disturbed... Your house and your kingdom will endure forever before me; your throne will be established forever. (2 Sam. 7:10,16; Psalm 89:29)

The people of Judah assumed this promise was unconditional. God had chosen Jerusalem, and placed his name there. The temple stood as a sign of God's eternal presence, and his promise to King David. The people were confident that God would never abandon Jerusalem and its people.

But they were assuming too much. Jeremiah warned the people of Judah not to take the goodness and patience of God for granted:

Reform your ways and your actions, and I will let you live in this place. Do not trust in deceptive words and say, "This is the temple of the Lord, the temple of the Lord, the temple of the Lord "(Jer. 7:3)

But the people clung to their delusions and stiffened their necks against the prophet's reproof. Jeremiah's prophesies of disaster for Jerusalem came to pass in 586 BC, when the armies of Babylon captured the city, destroyed the temple, and carried the Jews into captivity.

We have considered prophecies of judgment and promises of blessing. Now we come to a third kind of prophecy—prophecies of redemption through a coming Messiah.

CHRIST THE FULFILLMENT

Prophecies of redemption have their fulfillment in Christ. These prophecies remain open until they are fully realized in Christ.

The Samaritan woman at the well is one example. The story is told in John chapter four. Although a Samaritan and an outcast, Jesus saw in her a faith he had not found in Israel. This woman's amazing faith prompted her to tell Jesus: *"I know that Messiah is coming. When he comes, he will explain everything."* (John 4:25). Jesus told her: *"I am he."*

Where did this Samaritan woman get this idea of a Jewish messiah that would *explain everything* to the Samarians? The story of the Samaritans goes back centuries earlier.

The Samaritans were the descendents of the northern tribes of Israel who had escaped captivity when the Assyrians destroyed Samaria. They intermarried with foreigners whom the Assyrians had relocated in the vacated towns of the Israelites.

These immigrants were converted by Israelite priests to worship the God of Israel. But their knowledge of God was incomplete; they retained the idols brought from their lands. (The amazing story of their conversion is told in 2 Kings 17).

About this time Isaiah and Micah had a vision of Zion as a "light to the nations." Foreigners could come streaming to Zion to *learn the ways of the Lord, so they could walk in the Lord's path.* Swords would become plowshares and spears would become pruning hooks, and peace would reign. (Isa. 2; Mic.4)

Ezekiel, in exile in Babylon, caught the vision of Isaiah and Micah of Zion as a *light to the nations.* He gave these instructions to the Jews for when they returned to the land.

You are to distribute this land among yourselves according to the tribes of Israel. You are to allot it as an inheritance for yourselves and for **the aliens who have settled** *among you and who have children.*

You are to consider them the same as native-born Israelites; along with you they are to be allotted an inheritance among the tribes of Israel. In whatever tribe the alien settles, there you are to give him his inheritance, declares the Sovereign Lord. (Ezek. 47:21-23)

Non-Jews living in the land would become part of Israel. In this way, the restored temple would become *a house of prayer for all nations.*

But the Jewish returnees failed to embrace this vision. The books of Ezra-Nehemiah tells the story of a missed opportunity.

The Samaritans came to Jerusalem eager to help and learn. But the Jewish leaders were afraid that these "foreigners" would defile the Jewish religion. They mistakenly linked these seekers to the Canaanites of an earlier period of history.

The disappointed Samaritans complained to the

Persian rulers of the land, and work on the temple was suspended for 17 years. The Jewish returnees had turned these worshippers and potential allies into disillusioned, embittered enemies.

A century later, Ezra came to Jerusalem from Babylon. He was offended to learn that Jewish men had married non-Jewish women. He ordered all the Jewish men to divorce their non-Jewish wives. In the final chapter of Nehemiah we read: *They excluded from Israel all who were of foreign descent.* (Neh.13:3)

The result was four more centuries of hostility and strife. This hostile relationship between Jews and Samaritans was still at work when Jesus met the Samaritan woman at the well.

Ezra's generation missed an opportunity for a great blessing. They failed to see what Isaiah saw. But the vision did not go away. It was merely awaiting the Messiah who could look into the heart of a Samaritan woman and see a child of God.

Today, the story of Ezra's missed opportunity is being replayed in modern Israel. Ezekiel offered a vision of Israelis and Palestinians living together in peace, sharing the land of promise. So far, neither side has come to terms with this vision.

The vision remains open to those who have the faith and courage to take it to heart.

So let's sum up what can we learn from the divine potter:

- The future is open. Jesus' death and resurrection has opened a whole new set of potential futures for humanity.

- The curse of sin has been cancelled on the cross. No doom is inevitable; no good thing is impossible.
- Prophecy gives us glimpses of futures, but the outcome depends upon the choices we make.

Scripture hints at God's purpose for a humanity redeemed in Christ:

We know that when he appears, we shall be like him, for we shall see him as he is. (1 John 3:2)

We ourselves, who have the first fruits of the Spirit, groan inwardly as we wait eagerly for our adoption as sons, the redemption of our bodies. (Rom. 8:23)

All nations will come and worship before you, for your righteous acts have been revealed. (Rev. 15:4)

Yes, we can become a better people, not only as individuals, but as a nation. We can learn to *act justly, love mercy, and walk humbly with our God.* The way of peace can yet be found. Armageddon can be averted. The future is open.

While we are thinking of possibilities, let's look at another of Isaiah's wonderful visions that remain open in our time.

CHAPTER 3

A Highway to Assyria

Can you imagine peace in the Middle East?

I was in Jerusalem on November 17, 1977. I had just completed a teaching tour in Egypt and Jordan. Jerusalem was our last seminar. The rest of our team had left for home. I remained behind to pray and consider the next step of my ministry.

Then we got the news: Egyptian President Anwar Sadat was arriving in Jerusalem to address the Israeli Knesset. Sadat's historic visit confirmed my sense that God was calling us to ministry in Jerusalem. I went home and conferred with my wife, Willow.

One year later, we moved to Jerusalem to begin our ministry there. In March of 1979, we received word that President Carter would be coming to Jerusalem. Willow and I were invited to attend the Sunday church service with President and Mrs. Carter.

The signing of the Camp David treaty awakened us to a long overlooked passage in Isaiah 19:

In that day there will be a highway from Egypt to Assyria. The Assyrians will go to Egypt and the Egyptians will go to Assyria. The Egyptians and Assyrians will worship together. (Isa.19:23)

This passage begins as a prophecy against Egypt. In Isaiah's day, and for centuries, Egypt and Assyria were rival superpowers contending for regional dominance. Israel was caught in the middle, forced to pay tribute to one or the other or both.

But in verse 18, the tone of Isaiah's prophecy begins to shift. Isaiah's eyes are opened to see a new possibility. He sees in the Spirit an altar to the Lord set up in the heart of Egypt. Egyptians are offering sacrifices there and worshipping the Lord Almighty. The story unfolds:

So the Lord will make himself known to the Egyptians, and in that day they will acknowledge the Lord. (v. 21)

An oppressor afflicts Egypt, but God rescues them. They are smitten with plague, and the Lord heals them. Isaiah continues:

In that day there will be a highway from Egypt to Assyria. The Assyrians will go to Egypt and the Egyptians to Assyria. (v.23)

Can you imagine a peaceful Middle East? Jews and Arabs prospering together? Israelis and Palestinians sharing the land of promise? Commerce flowing freely from nation to nation? Impossible? Read on.

A few months after Camp David, Willow and I took another trip to Egypt. We traveled by Israeli bus to the border, where we changed to an Egyptian bus for the drive across the Sinai desert to Cairo (which took about 4 hours, not 40 years!)

From Cairo, we flew Egypt Air to Luxor. Snacks were served, so I pulled down my seatback tray. Someone had written "Shalom" on the tray in Hebrew, with a red marker pen. I knew then that Israeli tourists had preceded us.

In the Egyptian markets, shopkeepers kept calling out "Shalom, Shalom." They assumed that we were Israeli tourists and they were eager to have our business.

Israel, Egypt, and Jordan have already taken the first hesitant steps toward Isaiah's "highway to Assyria." Travel between Israel, Jordan, and Egypt is now commonplace.

The Egyptians and Assyrians will worship together. (v.23)

This part of Isaiah's vision came to pass centuries ago. The old gods of the Egyptians and Assyrians are long since dead and gone. Only the God of Abraham remains. (The Assyrian empire is also long gone. Their place has been taken by the people of Iraq, and Isaiah's vision is open to Iraqis as well.)

Judaism, Islam, and Christianity all have their roots in the faith of Abraham. All worship the same God, although they differ in particulars of belief and practice.

Jews may call God *Adonai* or *Elohim*. Muslims call God *Allah* as do Arabic-speaking Christians. (The Arabic Bible used throughout the Middle East translates *Elohim* as *Allah*, as does the Quran.) We call Elohim *God*. There are many languages, but only one God.

In Jerusalem, I studied Judaism and Islam under Jewish and Muslim teachers as part of my doctoral research. In Bethlehem, I taught Bible to Palestinian Christians at Bethlehem Bible College. My wife and I also operated an off-campus Friendship Center for Muslim university students.

With our Muslim friends, we discussed the Bible

and the Quran. We learned what the Quran said and Muslim people think about Jesus. They learned about Jesus, both from the New Testament, and from observing our day to day lives in Christ.

We discussed our differences frankly, but respectfully. We received respect in turn. We were often invited to their homes in the rural villages and refugee camps to meet their families. Every year we had a Christmas feast for our Muslim friends, who brought their families to celebrate the birth of Jesus with us.

Our objective was to break down barriers of misunderstanding. We discovered that misunderstandings went both ways. We learned that people of different religions can live together in mutual respect and consideration. I now believe that what Isaiah saw is possible, and is God's intention.

But too often, religion is exploited to feed dreams of conquest and domination by one group over another, thereby fueling the fires of hell. And this applies to "end time" scenarios that offer no other alternative than a bloody Armageddon. Isaiah had the better vision:

In that day Israel will be the third, along with Egypt and Assyria, a blessing in the earth. (v24)

Today, Israel is perceived in the Arab world as an unwelcome intruder and occupier of Arab lands. But Isaiah envisioned Israel as a valued trade partner with Egypt and Assyria, a *blessing in the earth.*

I can see this happening once Israelis and Palestinians learn how to share the land of promise. This would likely lead to some degree of economic integration between Israel and Palestine. In time this might lead to a common market, including at least Egypt, Israel, Palestine, and Jordan. The Lebanese would not want to be left out.

Impossible? It may seem that way, given the dismal lack of progress in the on-going peace process, and the history of antagonism between Israel and its Arab neighbors. But God is not finished with the people of the Middle East. And with God, nothing is impossible.

Sadly, many sincere Christians have been blinded by faulty interpretations of biblical prophecies and promises. They cannot see the vision that Isaiah saw. Instead, they urge Israel to be more aggressive and make no concessions toward the Palestinians. As Isaiah said, *The way of peace they do not know.* (Isa.59:8;Rom.3:17).

Isaiah concludes his vision:

The Lord Almighty will bless them saying, 'Blessed be Egypt my people, Assyria my handiwork, and Israel my inheritance. (v.25)

Yes, Israeli Jews are God's people. But so are the Egyptians, Palestinians, Syrians and Iraqis. There is a rabbinical story about the Israelites crossing the Red Sea. It goes like this:

Safe on the other side of the Red Sea, the Israelites begin to sing and dance, as they saw the Egyptians perishing in the sea.

In heaven, the angels saw the Israelites singing and dancing, and they too begin to sing and dance.

But the Lord rebuked them: "Those are also my people who are perishing in the sea, and you want to sing and dance?"

It was OK for the Israelites to sing and dance. They had just experienced a great deliverance. But God expected the angels to see from heaven's perspective. The angels should realize that God's love encompasses all peoples, and when one people suffers, God suffers with them.

How do we get to this *highway to Assyria?* The gate to this road is inscribed with Jesus' words, *Love your enemies.* We need to understand that our enemies are not necessarily God's enemies.

Of course there remain many obstacles to realizing Isaiah's vision. It may take several generations. But God is not running out of time.

Can this happen in our time? Or are we already into the "end time? We will take this question up in our next chapter, "End times and New Beginnings."

CHAPTER 4

End Times and New Beginnings
The End Time is not the end of time.

The plans of the Lord stand firm forever, the purposes of his heart through all generations. (Ps. 33:11)

People often ask me, "Are we living in the end time?" I would say, "It depends on what you are asking me."

If the question is, "Is this the time of Christ's return?" I would answer, "I don't know." No one knows, *Not the angels, nor the Son, but only the Father.*

If the question is, "Are we coming to the end of this age?" I would answer, "probably."

As a young man, I had been taught that we were living in the "last days," and that Christ's return was imminent. When most people ask me about the "end time" they are assuming that there is only one "end time." I hear people talking about "the end of time" or "the end of history."

But a lifetime of biblical study has led me to see this question in a different light. I see in biblical history that generation follows generation, and age follows age. And every age has its own "end time."

The world is not going to end any time soon. Scripture tells us that God's love extends to a thousand generations. Some 150 generations have passed since that was written. We still have a long way to go.

THE FOUR GENERATION CYCLE

Punishing the sins of the fathers to the third and fourth generation of those who hate me, but showing love to a thousand generations of those who love me. (Deut. 5:9).

The story of the Bible is a story of generations. There are usually four generations living at any one time—The father's generation, the children's, the grandchildren's, and the great-grandchildren's.

One generation is always passing away, another is moving into leadership as elders, the next is raising their families, and the next is being born. Deuteronomy tells us that a powerful man may continue to influence his descendents as long as he lives.

This could be for up to four generations. His death marks the end of an era for his family. This four generation cycle can be seen throughout the Old Testament.

Joseph was the fourth generation starting with Abraham. In Joseph's time, The Age of the Patriarch's ended in a famine which drove the family from the land of promise into Egypt.

Joseph's death began a new crisis era for Israel. Exodus begins with the observation:

Now Joseph and all his brothers and that generation died...then a new king, who did not know Joseph, came to power in Egypt. (Exod.1:6,8)

32

Joshua was the fourth generation from Joseph. The Exodus took place in Joshua's time. But the generation of adults that left Egypt did not have the faith to go into the promised land. Except for Joshua and Caleb, they all died in the wilderness. Joshua led Israel into the promised land, and we read:

Israel served the Lord throughout the lifetime of Joshua and of the elders who outlived him. (Jos.24:31)

After that whole generation had been gathered to their fathers, another generation grew up, who neither knew the Lord nor what he had done for Israel. (Judg. 2:10)

Joshua's death marked the end of an age for Israel. But this four generation pattern continued through the Judges into the time of the kings. Saul, David, Solomon, and Rehoboam reigned over all Israel.

Rehoboam's reign brought an end to the united Kingdom of Israel. During his reign, the northern tribes broke away. The kingdom was split into a northern kingdom called **Israel**, and a southern kingdom called **Judah**.

After a period of instability in Israel, the Lord promised King Jehu that he and his descendents would reign for four generations. That period of stability ended when Jehu's great grandson Jeroboam II died. (2 Kings 10: 30;15:1)

The four generation cycle in American history. Strauss and Howe have discerned this same cycle in American history. They noticed that with every three or four generations there is a national "crisis era." (Strauss 1997)

Of course, crises happen in every generation, but

these fourth generation crises differ in intensity, extent, and far reaching consequences. They bring one age to a close and begin another.

According to Strauss and Howe, these crisis eras begin with some sudden calamity that shocks and changes the mood of the nation. One crisis cascades into another, until they all pile up into a final decisive crisis that determines the fate of the nation.

The last such "crisis era" began with the Great Depression in 1929, and concluded with World War II. The previous crisis era concluded with the Civil War. And the Revolutionary War before that. (Strauss 1997)

This four generation cycle is one of the great patterns of history. Every third or fourth generation seems to mark the end of one "age" and the beginning of another. Each of these ages ends with a time of convulsive change. In such times the foundations of society are shaken, and old certainties are called into question. As the poet Yeats wrote: "Things fall apart; the centre cannot hold."

To the people living through these crisis eras, it may seem like the end of the world. But what seems to be the end of everything, proves instead to be a new beginning.

The prophets had several terms for these crisis eras that occur and reoccur in biblical history. They called them:

- **The last days**.
- **The time of the end**.
- **The day of the Lord**.

Today, people think of these as eschatological sayings about the Second Coming or the End of the World. But the biblical record tells us that the prophets were speaking of events that happened long ago in biblical history.

THE LAST DAYS

*In the **last days** the mountain of the Lord's temple will be established...all nations will stream to it...they will beat their swords into plowshares and their spears into pruning hooks.* (Isa.2; Mic. 4)

*Afterward, the Israelites will return and seek the Lord their God and David their king. They will come trembling to the Lord and to his blessings in the **last days**.* (Hos. 3:5)

In the Old Testament, the expression *the last days* often simply meant "at some later time." It did not imply that time itself would end. Isaiah, Micah, and Hosea saw, not the "end of the world," but the end of one age, and the beginning of another.

The term *last days* often has a pleasant connotation. It represents a time when the crisis is past, and *times of refreshing come from the presence of the Lord.* As Peter announced on the day of Pentecost:

*This is what was spoken by the prophet Joel, 'In the **last days**,' God says, 'I will pour out my Spirit on all people... before the great and glorious day of the Lord. And everyone who calls on the name of the Lord will be saved.* (Acts 2:17-22)

The writer of Hebrews also believed that the apos-

35

tles were living in the **last days** when he wrote: *In these **last days** God has spoken to us by his Son.* (Heb 1:2)

But the "last days" can have a negative connotation as well. The apostles sensed that their age was coming to an end. They warned of a darker time to follow:

But mark this: There will be terrible times in the last days. People will be lovers of themselves, lovers of money... (2 Tim. 3:1)

*You must understand that in the **last days** scoffers will come, scoffing and following their own evil desires.* (2 Pet.3:3)

These last days are days of opportunity. But they have their dangers as well.

THE TIME OF THE END

The "End Time," is not a strictly biblical term. Daniel does make three references to a *time of the end*. In Daniel chapter 8, Daniel had a vision of a ram with two horns. This ram was attacked by a goat with one "prominent horn." He is told: T*he vision concerns the **time of the end**.*(Dan 8:17)

Later in this chapter we are told that the two headed Ram referred to the Medes and Persians. The goat with the large horn referred to the Greeks of Alexander the Great.(v.20)

This *time of the end* referred to the defeat of Persia by the army of Alexander the Great, around 331 BC. This was another crisis time for Jews under Persia rule.

The next reference to the *time of the end* is in Daniel chapter 11.

*At **the time of the end** the king of the south will engage him in battle, and the king of the North will storm out against him.* (Dan 11:40)

After Alexander died in 326 BC, his empire was divided among his four generals. General Seleucus acquired the eastern part of the empire, and established his capital in Antioch, Syria. General Ptolemy acquired the western part, and established his capital in Alexandria, Egypt.

Most commentaries identify the king of the south with the Ptolemy dynasty in Egypt, and the king of the north with the Seleucid dynasty in Syria. The Jews would be caught in the middle between these two rivals. This time of trouble will be discussed in a later chapter.

The last reference is found in Daniel 12:

*He replied, "Go your way, Daniel, because the words are closed up and sealed until the **time of the end**."* (Dan.12:9)

The times depicted in Daniel's vision began around 167 BC, with the desecration of the temple in Jerusalem. The actual book of Daniel was probably written around this same time. We will revisit Daniel in later chapters of my book. These are the only references in the Bible to a *time of the end*.

THE DAY OF THE LORD

*Woe to you who long for the **day of the Lord**!*

*Why do you long for the **day of the Lord**? That day will be darkness, not light.* (Amos 5:18)

The people of Israel in Amos' day had the wrong idea about the *day of the Lord*. They saw it as a time when God would rise up and destroy their enemies. Amos was telling the people that God's judgment was coming.

He begins his book with a list of Israel's neighbors who are marked for judgment. I can imagine his hearers shouting, "Yes, brother, preach it!" as he catalogues the sins of Israel's neighbors and pronounces their doom.

Then they get very quiet when he starts listing the sins of Israel, and tells them what God has in store for Israel:

An enemy will overrun the land; he will put down your strongholds and plunder your fortresses...on that day I will punish Israel for her sins. (Amos. 4:11,14)

There are several other references to the *day of the Lord*. The first concerned Judah and Jerusalem:

*Be silent before the Sovereign Lord, for the day of the Lord is near...The Great **day of the Lord** is near and coming quickly.* (Zech.1:7,14;2:3).

That day came in 586 BC, when the Babylonians destroyed the city and the temple and carried the Jews into exile. The Edomites would be next to face the day of the Lord, as **Obadiah** prophesied:

*The **day of the Lord** is near for all nations. As you have done, it will be done to you.* (Obad. v15).

That judgment also came at the hands of the Babylonians. The next reference concerned the Egyptians and its allies:

*Wail and say, "Alas for that day!" the **day of the Lord** is near, a day of clouds, a time of doom for the nations.* Ezek. 30:3)

Their doom would also come at the hands of Babylon, in 564 BC. Next came Joel's prophecy to the Jews of Judea:

*Alas for that day! For the **day of the Lord** is near; it will come as a destruction from the Almighty.* (Joel 1:15; 2:1,31).

In Joel, the *day of the Lord* came as a prolonged drought and a locust infestation. (I place Joel in this period because there was no king, only priests and elders).

Malachi later prophesied: *See, I will send you the prophet Elijah before that great and dreadful **day of the Lord** comes.* (Mal. 4:5).

Jesus relates Malachi's prophecy to the coming of John the Baptist. (Matt. 17:12).

We see from biblical history that the *day of the Lord* is **not the end of the world**. Nor is it a one-time event. God is still judging the nations. America is not exempt from that judgment. *Our day of the Lord* will surely come.

When? How? I don't know. What will be the outcome? That too is unknowable.

Not only nations, but every individual also has his or her personal *day of the Lord.*

For we must all appear before the judgment seat of Christ, that each one may receive what is due him... Man is destined to die once, and after that the judgment. (2 Cor. 5:10; Heb. 9:27)

The *day of the Lord* is never more than a heart-beat and last breath away.

ARE WE LIVING IN THE 'END TIME?'

I suspect this present post-World War II age is coming into its "end time." Strauss and Howe in 1997 expected the next crisis era to begin around 2005. It may have come a little sooner than expected. (Strauss 1997)

It probably began with the terrorist attack of September 11, 2001. The inconclusive Iraq and Afghanistan wars, the financial crisis in 2008, and the current recession are a continuation of this crisis. The outcome of this crisis era is still over our horizon.

What we can predict is that generation will follow generation. The oldest generation will die off without seeing the conclusion of this era. But younger generations will live to see the dawning of a new era. What that new day will be like, no one knows.

We can know this: Every age has its own "end time." Every "end time" contains within it a new beginning. The seeds of that new beginning are already being planted. Nothing that is born of the Spirit is lost in the process.

In our next chapter, **The Four Winds of Heaven**, we will look deeper at the eras that make up the four generational cycle. Hopefully, this will enable us to better know what to expect in the months and years just ahead.

CHAPTER 5

The Four Winds of Heaven
The shifting winds of change.

It was the last day of Sukkoth, the Festival of Booths. A crowd gathered in the courtyard of the temple. They watched anxiously to see which way the smoke bent in the wind as it ascended from the sacrifice on the altar. (Schauss 1938)

This was an annual event in Jesus' day. Jesus himself might have been among the crowd of watchers. In those days, people believed that the direction of the wind on this occasion was an omen for the coming year.

The smoke bending northward (a south wind) was seen as an omen of scarcity. The rich merchants would benefit from high prices. But it meant low income for the poor peasants, in a year of high prices. The poor were sad; the rich were glad.

The smoke bending eastward (a west wind) brought sighs of relief from the crowd. On this occasion, it was an omen of abundant crops in the coming year. Everybody, rich or poor, was happy to see the west wind.

The smoke bending southward (a north wind) was considered a good omen for the poor, for it pointed to good harvests. But for the merchants, it meant low prices and profits. The poor were glad; the merchants sad.

But the smoke bending westward (an east wind) was the worst omen for rich and poor alike. It pointed to a year of famine. The rich were sad—nothing to sell. The poor were sad—no money to buy anything, and no crops in the field. Everyone dreaded an "east wind" year.

I doubt if Jesus believed in these omens. But he did use the wind and weather as a metaphor for discerning the times and seasons. On one occasion he told the crowd:

When you see a cloud rising from the west, immediately you say, "It's going to rain," and it does. And when the south wind blows, you say, "It's going to be hot," and it is ...Hypocrites! You know how to interpret the appearance of the earth and sky. How is it that you don't know how to interpret this present time? (Luke 12:54-56)

*Wind make*s a good metaphor for the work of the Spirit, because *wind* and *spirit* are often the same word (RUACH) in Hebrew. Notice how Jesus used wind and spirit in his conversation with Nicodemus:

*The **wind** blows wherever it pleases. You hear its sound, but you cannot tell where it comes from or where it is going. So is everyone born of the **Spirit.*** (John 3:8)

Jesus' ministry was a new wind of the Spirit blowing across the land. *"The time is at hand,"* Jesus declared, *"The kingdom of God is near."* (Mark 1:8).

42

We will explore the *four winds* as metaphors used in biblical prophecy. Then we should be able to better discern how the wind is blowing in our world today. These metaphors are:

1. Shifting winds by generation.
2. Ezekiel's valley of the dry bones.
3. The rise and fall of world empires.
4. The harvest of the ages.

(I will be basing these metaphors on the climate and seasons of Israel).

SHIFTING WINDS BY GENERATION

There is a cultural wind shift as each new generation comes of age. Each generation brings its own distinctive fashion, cultural icons, and mood. The German word for this is "zeitgeist," or the "spirit of the age."

I am using "era" here to refer to periods identified by a particular generation, like the "Boomers" or "Generation X." Most of these eras last for some 20-25 years, until the next generation comes along and brings in a new era. Remember "the age of Aquarius?"

Each era's particular cultural and spiritual flavor is created from the spirit of the age interacting with God's Spirit.

I am using "age" here in a special sense to mean the four generation cycle we discussed in the previous chapter. In this sense, there are usually four eras to an age.

South wind eras. Jesus said: *When the south wind blows, you say, "It's going to be hot."* The south wind brings the warm, drowsy summer days that ripen the crops in the field and the fruit on the trees. It represents times of national peace, prosperity, and rebuilding.

The post-World War II boom of the 1950's may have been a *south wind* era for the USA. Spiritually, it was a time of rather conventional values. Young post-war families were flocking to new subdivisions in the suburbs. New churches were being built to accommodate these families.

We may have our own personal *south wind* times. These are the more settled and mature times of our life, quiet times that allow *the fruit of the Spirit* to ripen.

West wind eras. Jesus said: *When you see a cloud rising from the west, immediately you say, "It's going to rain," and it does.* The west wind comes laden with moisture from the Mediterranean Sea. It brings the steady winter rains, so essential to agriculture in Israel. In summer, it is cool and dry, bringing a welcome respite from the heat.

The *west wind* represents times of spiritual refreshing and renewal. As Joel prophesied:

He sends you abundant showers, both autumn and spring rains, as before. The threshing floor will be filled with grain; the vats will overflow with the new wind and oil. (Joel 2:23)

I will pour out my Spirit on all people, your sons and daughters will prophecy, your old men will dream dreams." (Joel. 2:28)

44

The impact of the *west wind* on society is both secular and religious. The 1960's and 1970's may have been a *west wind* era. It began with the excitement of the Kennedy election. Woodstock, hippies and flower children, drugs, cults and communes, and Vietnam war protests were all part of the spirit of the age.

Meanwhile, the Spirit of God was blowing through the church. Pope John XXIII and Vatican II opened the windows of the Catholic Church to the fresh wind of the Spirit. Catholic and Protestant churches were swept by Charismatic Renewal. Hippies and flower children became "Jesus People." Drugs gave way to speaking in tongues.

North wind eras. The north wind is cold, wet, and blustery. It often comes with peals of thunder and flashes of lightning. It is an unpleasant wind, as inferred in the proverb: *As a north wind brings rain, so a sly tongue brings angry looks.* (Prov. 25:23)

In a *north wind* era, people have the sense that the institutions of society are falling apart, and the government is clueless and inept. "Government is not the solution; it is the problem" is a north wind mantra.

This widespread feeling of ennui persists even when people are doing well. Strauss and Howe describe these eras as an "unraveling." (Strauss)

The 1980's were a transition time, with the spiritual wind shifting between west and north. Charismatic Renewal gave way to mega churches and culture wars. A backlash from Vatican II brought forward more conservative popes.

In the 1990's the shift to a north wind was more

pronounced. The top tiers of our society gained great wealth, while the wages of the middle class stagnated. The gap between rich and poor widened as the twentieth century came to a close. Marriages unraveled as well.

East wind eras. In summer, the wind comes from off the desert, blazing hot, and laden with dust and sand. The dust penetrates the walls, grits in the teeth, and makes the eyes itch. Tempers get short as the temperature soars. Fortunately these "khamsin" winds usually last only a few days.

The *east wind* is a metaphor for times of God's judgment. It is the "end time" that brings each age to its close, and sets the stage for the incoming age.

Even though he (Ephraim) thrives among his brothers, an **east wind** *from the Lord will come, blowing in from the desert.* (Hos.13:15)

The **east wind** *carries him (the wicked) off, and he is gone.* (Job. 27:21)

In Exodus, it was the east wind that scorched the grain, creating the seven years of famine. The east wind also brought the locusts which plagued the Egyptians.

The *east wind* can bring both deliverance and judgment. It was the east wind that pushed back the waters of the Red Sea, creating a path of escape for the Israelites, but a lethal, watery trap for the Egyptian army.

The *east wind* tends to disrupt those plans of man which are contrary to the plans of God. We read in Psalm 49: *You destroyed the ships of Tarshish, shattered by an east wind.* (Ps 48:9)

46

There is an interesting story behind this verse. King Jehoshaphat of Judah and King Ahaziah of Israel formed a trading partnership. They built a fleet of ships to carry gold from Africa. They were hoping through the gold trade to revive the wealth and glory of Solomon's day. (1 Kings 22:41; 2 Chron.20:35)

But they did not consult the Lord before launching this venture. A violent east wind wrecked the ships before they ever left port, just as the Psalm says.

In our four generation cycle, the east wind brings in the crisis eras that mark the end of one age and the beginning of another. Since they come around about every fourth generation, anyone who lives a full lifespan will probably experience one of these east wind times.

I was a small child when World War II started. I am now a great-grandfather. It may be time for another *east wind* season.

Of course, the wind does not blow steadily in one direction all the time. In any era, there will be localized gusts of wind from different directions. There are also overlaps between eras, when it is more difficult to discern which way the wind is blowing.

THE VALLEY OF DRY BONES

*Come from the **four winds**, O breath, and breathe upon these slain, that they may live. So I prophesied as he commanded me, and breath entered into them; they came to life and stood up on their feet - a vast army.*

I will put my Spirit in you and you will live, and I will settle you in your own land. Then you will know that I the Lord has spoken and I have done it. (Ezek 37: 9,10, 14)

Ezekiel had a vision of a valley full of dry bones. The dry and scattered bones represents the Jewish people during the Babylonian exile. The gathering and reconnecting of these bones represents the Jews returning to Jerusalem to rebuild their national life. The story of this return is told in Ezra and Nehemiah.

Ezekiel's concern was for the spiritual life of the Jewish community. Hence his calls for the *four winds* to breathe the life of the Spirit into the Jewish people.

All *four winds of heaven* can be seen in the history of this story. The first Jews set out for the land of promise. There was the excitement of laying of a new temple in Jerusalem.

But this gave way to disappointment and frustration as the work was halted by the Persians for seventeen years. Then joy returned as **Haggai** and **Zechariah** prophesied, and the temple was finally completed.

Then a time of hardship followed. There was a deep economic recession. The book of Joel seems to belong to this period. Joel describes a persistent drought followed by a locust plague. There is no mention of a king, only priests and elders as leaders.

A century later, joy returned with the arrival of Ezra with the *Book of the Law*. Finally we have the prophecies of Malachi, closing out this period of history.

Four centuries of prophetic silence would follow.

Midway through this period would come the terrors of Antiochus IV and the courage of the Maccabees.

The four winds continued to blow throughout these long centuries. Generations were born and died.

Then came John the Baptist preaching, *the time has come; the kingdom of God is near.* Jesus followed, announcing *The Spirit of the Lord God is upon me.*

The west wind was beginning to blow again over the land of Israel.

But Daniel offers still another metaphor using the *four winds of heaven.*

THE RISE AND FALL OF WORLD EMPIRES

*In my vision at night I looked, and there before me were **four winds of heaven**, churning up the great sea. Four beasts, each different from the others, came up out of the sea.* (Dan. 7: 2,3)

The winds of change create great turbulence in human history. The kingdoms of this world do not passively yield to the kingdom of God. The spirit of the age reacts violently to the Spirit of God. As Jesus said:

From the days of John the Baptist until now, the kingdom of heaven has been forcefully advancing, and forceful men lay hold of it. (Matt.11:12)

All kinds of beasts can be dredged up out of our human capacity for evil. Even our best intentions often lead to unintended results. Some of the worst of these monsters come dressed in religious garb.

49

In Daniel's vision, the beasts were a succession of world empires that contended with each other for dominance in the Middle East. These beastly empires correspond to Nebuchadnezzar's dream of a statue with a golden head. (Daniel 2).

The four empires are usually identified as Babylon, Persia, the Greeks of Alexander the Great, and the Seleucid-Ptolemy regimes that followed Alexander's death. (Some scholars refer to Rome as the fourth beast).

Daniel sees that these beasts *had been stripped of their authority, but were allowed to live for a period of time.* In other words, they had lost their empires but their ideas, culture, and technological advances lived on in successive empires. (Dan. 7:12)

In Revelation, John combines these four beasts into one beast with seven heads and ten horns. John may have added Egypt, Assyria, and Rome to Daniel's four beasts to make up the seven heads of his beast.

The ten horns may represent smaller neighboring kingdoms swallowed up by these world empires. The exact identity of these horns and heads is not critical to our story. (See Jeremiah 46-49 for a possible list)

John sees Rome as the incarnation of all the beastly empires that preceded it. It is also a symbol of all the beasts that have followed through the ages.

The Roman Empire finally came to its end in 476 AD. But beastly empires continue to rise out of the human drive for world domination. In every generation, people worship the beast of imperialism, saying, *Who is like the beast? Who can make war against the beast.* (Rev 11:4)

This Beast certainly knows how to recruit the religions of the world to serve its interests. In Revelation, *the great prostitute sitting on the beast*, and the *false prophet* are images of an unholy union of **Religion and State**, working together for worldly power and privilege. (Rev. 17-18)

For John, these images called to mind Rome, Jerusalem, and the Roman-appointed High Priest and his clique. The imagery comes from Isaiah's prophecy against Jerusalem:

See how the faithful city has become a harlot! She once was full of justice; righteousness used to dwell in her—but now murderers. (Isa.1:21)

Religion, including our own, is still highly susceptible to this temptation— serving the agenda of the State while reaping the benefits of privilege, position, and influence.

A DEEPER MYSTERY

Daniel and Revelation depict these world empires as "beastly." But the picture is not all dark. Each of these empires has contributed something of value during their time. Jews in exile were responsible for many of these contributions.

Judaism also benefited from these experiences. Their horizons were expanded and their world-view enlarged as they came in contact with new ideas. The result was a cross-fertilization of ideas that enriched Judaism, and by extension, the Christian faith. In this way, the Jewish experience became scattered seed, enriching the whole world.

For example, in Persia, Jews came into contact with the religion of Zoroaster. These contacts stimulated new thinking about the Messiah, the resurrection of the dead, and the nature of evil powers, for these are all elements of Zoroastrianism.

The Magi, who came bearing gifts for the Christ Child, were probably Zoroastrian priests. Matthew's story of the Magi may be his subtle way of recognizing the contribution of that religion to Judaism, and from Judaism to the Christian faith.

And the Magi, bowing at the feet of the baby Jesus, remind us that **all knowledge and truth must ultimately bow at the feet of the risen Christ**.

It is the work of the Spirit to sift out those elements of civilization that are toxic, and refine those which represent an advance in the Kingdom of God. This doesn't happen all at once. The *winds of heaven* have continued to blow through the ages and generations.

We still have one more metaphor of the *four winds* to consider.

THE HARVEST OF THE AGES

*At that time men will see the Son of Man coming in clouds with great power and glory. And he will send his angels and gather his elect from the **four winds**, from the ends of the earth to the ends of heaven.* (Mk 13:26)

I will discuss the *Son of Man coming in clouds* in the final chapter of this book. For now, let us focus on the *four winds* and the *gathering of the elect*. It takes all four seasons, and all four *winds of heaven,* to produce a harvest. The winter cold, the spring rains, the summer heat all contribute what is needful for the harvest. Not all of the harvest takes place in the autumn. The barley is harvested in the Spring. The wheat, is harvested later, in early summer. The orchard fruit is picked later in the Summer. Then the grapes, and lastly in November, the olives are picked.

So it is with the harvest of the ages. It is a process of cultivating, sowing, watering, and harvesting. Jesus told his disciples:

Thus the saying, "One sows and another reaps is true." I sent you to reap what you have not worked for. Others have done the hard work, and you have reaped the benefits of their labor. (John 4:38)

Generations of Jews in exile sowed their seeds of enlightenment in the Gentile world. Soon it would be the apostles' turn. They would reap what earlier generations had sown. And they would plant seeds for future generations to reap. This process of sowing and reaping continues to this day.

Every age has its own end time, as Jesus said, *The harvest is at the end of the age.* In these end times, the *wheat is gathered into the barn,* and the *weeds are pulled up and put into the fire.* (Matt.13:39,40)

Age by Age, God's people are being *gathered together unto Him... from the ends of the earth to the ends of heaven.* (2 Th.2:1; Matt. 24:31)

53

TODAY'S PREVAILING WIND

The attack of September 11, 2001, may have been a gust of a coming *east wind* era. For several years, the wind has been veering back and forth between a *north wind* and an *east wind* era. Given the current economic distress, it now seems that the *east wind* has become the prevailing wind of this era.

God is working in this *east wind* era, as in all other times. He is calling people to the harvest field, to *gather his wheat into the barn,* while *the chaff are burned with an unquenchable fire.* (Matt.13:12)

There is a lot of chaff in our culture and society. Much of our great national wealth and power looks like gold, but is nothing more than "wood, straw, and stubble." These will soon be tested by fire. The Iraq War has already exposed the limits of our power to impose our will on the world. We are certainly in for a time of testing.

But nothing born of the Spirit will perish. That which is of God will emerge from the fire refined and revealed as the true gold, silver, and precious stones. We will emerge as a changed, and perhaps chastened nation.

This is our time. *Whoever watches the wind will not plant; whoever looks at the clouds will not reap.* (Eccl. 11:4)

We don't get to choose the times in which we live. We must live with what we are given. We can't put our lives on hold, waiting for some better time. The future is always uncertain. Jeremiah has a word for times like these. It is the same word he gave to the Jews going into exile in Babylon.

Build houses and settle down; plant gardens and eat what they produce. Marry and have sons and daughters in marriage, so that they too may have sons and daughters. Increase in numbers there; do not decrease. (Jer. 29:5)

And remember, this is not the end of the world. For what often seems to be the end, is really a new beginning. If I don't see that new beginning, my children or grandchildren will. I have faith.

CHAPTER 6

A Dark Night on the Mount of Olives

When will all this happen?

Five men huddled in the dark, on the western slopes of the Mount of Olives. One of these five men was Jesus.

Across the narrow Kidron valley, they could see the walls of Jerusalem, and high above the walls, the holy temple of the Jewish people.

There was a sharp chill in the night air, but it was too dangerous to build a fire. Even a small fire could be seen by the guards stationed on the city walls. For in the city, powerful men were plotting the death of Jesus. They were afraid to move against him in daylight, because of Jesus' popularity among the people.

But Jesus and his disciples were not in the city that night. They had slipped away at dusk to a safe house in a village on the eastern slopes of the Mount of Olives.

Jesus could not sleep. He sensed that the hour of his death was at hand. In his mind he could see the ominous shadow of a Roman cross. Not wanting to disturb his sleeping disciples, he slipped away quietly to pray.

Also unable to sleep were four of Jesus' disciples— Peter, Andrew, James and John. They were kept awake by something Jesus had said earlier, as they were leaving the temple complex:

Do you see all these great buildings? Not one stone here will be left on another; every stone will be thrown down. (Mark 13:2)

The temple was to be destroyed again? Actually, this was the second temple to stand on this holy site. The first temple, built by Solomon, was destroyed by the Babylonians in 586 BC. It was rebuilt in 521 BC by Jews returning from the Babylonian exile.

In 20 BC, Herod the Great launched a massive remodeling and expansion of the temple complex. This project was still underway in Jesus' time. It would require another 20 years to complete the project, just in time for it to be destroyed again.

Jesus had a vision of this temple in ruins, shrouded by smoke from a burning city. In his mind's eye, he saw the temple's defenders sprawled in death. He saw a cruel army pulling down the stones of the temple, tumbling them down into the valley below. It was a terrible, horrifying vision.

Perhaps it was triggered by an event earlier that week. Jesus had confronted the moneychangers and animal sellers from the Court of the Gentiles of the temple. He declared:

My house will be called a house of prayer for all nations, but you have made it a den of thieves. (Mark 11:17)

The *house of prayer* was a quote from Isaiah. In the original temple, foreigners and the physically impaired were excluded. But Isaiah foresaw a new temple, where no one would be excluded. It would be a place where foreigners could come and worship and find *joy in my house of prayer...a house of prayer for all nations.* (Isa.56:7)

The den of thieves was a quote from Jeremiah. Jeremiah protested against those who oppressed the alien, the fatherless, and the widow, and shed innocent blood, while boasting of their devotion to the temple. Jeremiah asked:

Has this house which bears my Name become a den of thieves to you?... I will thrust you from my presence. (Jer.7:11,15)

Since the time of the Maccabees, the office of High Priest had fallen in disrepute. The office had been bought and sold, obtained by political manipulation, and even by murder.

In 67 BC, one rival for the High Priesthood gained the backing of the Romans. From that time on, the High Priest was a Roman appointee. The Sadducees were his party. The Sadducees did not accept the prophetic books as scripture. So they had no regard for Isaiah's vision of an inclusive temple.

They did not think of the temple as a *house of prayer for all nations.* Instead, they saw it as a source of money, privilege, and power. The temple's Court of the Gentiles had become a profit center.

Jesus driving out the moneychangers was his prophetic judgment against the corrupt high priesthood that would bring down God's wrath upon Jerusalem and the temple.

THE DISCIPLES' QUESTION

The disciples were stunned by Jesus' prediction that the temple would be destroyed again. The four sleepless disciples went out into the night in search of Jesus. When they found him, they asked:

Tell us, when will these things happen? And what will be the sign that they are all about to happen? (Mark.13:4)

Note that this is a two part question:

1. They wanted to know when to expect this destruction of the temple.
2. They wanted a sign that would warn them that this calamity was imminent.

We can fast-forward to the end of this discourse to get Jesus' answer to the "when" part of this question.

*I tell you the truth, **this generation** will certainly not pass away until all these things have happened.* (Mark 13:30)

Jesus was not predicting events of our time thousands of years in the future. He was describing what would happen within the disciples' generation, as he told the religious authorities earlier that week:

*I tell you the truth, all this will come upon **this generation**. O Jerusalem, Jerusalem, you who kill the prophets... Look, your house is left to you desolate.* (Matt. 23: 35-36)

This destruction did happen within that generation, just as Jesus said. But first, the disciples had a mission to accomplish. That mission was to declare the gospel to the nations. In the next 45 years, they would be planting the seed for ages to come.

Jesus wanted to prepare the disciples for the challenges ahead as they carried out their gospel mission. He told them:

Don't be deceived. The first thing Jesus told his disciples was, *Watch out that no one deceives you.*

The apostles would encounter many deceivers, false messiahs, and false prophets in the course of their mission. Luke in Acts records two such instances:

- Peter and John encountered Simon the Sorcerer in Samaria, who tried to buy apostolic authority from Peter and John. (Acts 8)
- Paul encountered the false prophet Bar-Jesus, whom Paul encountered on the Island of Cyprus. (Acts 13)

Don't be distracted. *When you hear of wars and rumors of wars, do not be alarmed. There will be earthquakes in various places, and famines.* (Luke adds *pestilences* to this list).

With each calamity, deceivers will claim, *The time is near.* But Jesus tells his disciples, *Do not follow them.* (Luke 21:8)

These are **not signs** of the end time. These things have happened since the beginning of time, would continue to happen throughout history, and still happen today. Jesus said, *These things must happen, but the end is still to come.*

Don't be deterred by the opposition. The apostles would face rejection, betrayal and persecution. *On account of me, you will stand before governors and kings as witnesses to them.* (v.9-13)

All of these things happened in the days of the apostles. In Acts, we read of Peter and John standing before the Sanhedrin, enduring beatings for Christ's sake. Paul stood before Governors Felix and Festus, King Agrippa, and Nero Caesar, bearing witness of his faith in Jesus Christ.

None of these obstacles would prevent the apostles from accomplishing their mission. Jesus said, *The gospel must be preached to all nations.* (Mark 13:10)

Peter and Paul would both die in Nero's persecution, about 66 AD. Paul's death would signal the beginning of the end of that era. For 66 AD would see the opening battles of the Jewish-Roman war. This war would conclude with the destruction of the temple in 70 AD.

Jesus then took up the second part of the disciples' question: *What will be the sign that they are all about to happen?*

THE ABOMINATION THAT CAUSES DESOLATION

When you see 'the abomination that causes desolation' standing where it does not belong—let the reader understand—then let those who are in Judea flee to the mountains. (Mark. 13:14)

This would be the sign that would tell Jewish believers in Judea that the destruction of the temple was imminent. Let us note some variations in Matthew, Mark, and Luke's accounts.

*Let the **reader** understand.* This is obviously an editorial note added by Mark and Matthew for the benefit of their readers. Jesus was **talking**, not writing, to the four disciples in the dark of night. Matthew added the words, s*poken through the prophet Daniel,* to ensure that his readers would get the reference.

Jesus' disciples would have recognized the *abomination* quote as from Daniel 9 and 1 Maccabees 1. The date of this abomination was 167 BC.

1 Maccabees tells of a reign of terror in Jerusalem carried out by the Seleucid King Antiochus IV, who tried to stamp out the Jewish religion. The king issued orders that required all Jews in Judea to:

*Break the Sabbaths and profane the feasts and pollute the sanctuary and the sanctified; to build altars and sacred precincts and idol temples, and sacrifice hogs and unclean cattle...On the fifteenth day of Chislev in the year one hundred and forty-five (167 BC), the king erected the **abomination of desolation** above the altar.*(1 Macc.1:54)

These dreadful events triggered a Jewish uprising, led by the family known as the Maccabees (Hammers). These Jewish fighters succeeded in liberating the temple after a bloody three and a half year struggle. The Jewish festival Hanukah commemorates the re-dedication of the temple following these events.

Jesus was telling his disciples that history would

repeat itself. Once again, there would be conflict over the temple in Jerusalem. There would be another Jewish uprising against foreign occupation. Once again pagan armies would desecrate the temple in Jerusalem.

The Zealots would lead the Jewish people into another war with Rome. But this time, there would be no miraculous deliverance.

Jesus did not want any believers in Judea to get trapped in this holocaust. He told them: *Then let those who are in Judea flee to the mountains.* (Matt. 24:6)

There is a time to stand fast in the face of danger, and to persevere in the face of hardship. As Jesus said, *As long as it is day, we must do the work of him who sent me.* (John 9:4)

And there is a time to get out of a bad situation. Jesus said, *Night is coming when no man can work.* Night was coming for Jesus' followers in Jerusalem and Judea.

Please note that these instructions were **only** for believers still living **in Judea**. By the time this happened, Christian churches would be established throughout the Roman empire. Jesus was not suggesting that all believers everywhere should flee to the mountains.

Luke did not use the *abomination* quote from Daniel. His Gentile readers might not have recognized the source of the quote. Instead, he used plain language: *When you see Jerusalem surrounded by armies, you will know that its **desolation is near.*** (Luke. 21:20)

THE GREAT TRIBULATION

Jesus then began to describe the terrible events that would occur during the final months of the siege of Jerusalem, in 69 and 70 BC.

*How dreadful it will be in those days for pregnant women and nursing mothers! Pray that this will take place in the winter, because those will be days of **distress** unequaled from the beginning, when God created the world, until now— and never to be equaled again.* (Mark 13:18-19)

Matthew in the King James Version renders *distress* as *great tribulation*. The Greek word means "trouble" or "great stress."

Many Christians worry about missing the Rapture and having to go through the *great tribulation*. This passage is used as a "proof text" in many end time scenarios.

But nothing in scripture says that this *tribulation* will take place between the Rapture and the Second Coming of Christ, or that it will last for seven years. This is simply assumed in Darby's dispensational system.

In fact, Jesus did set a time frame for this *great tribulation*. He said it would happen within that generation. And so it did, almost 2000 years ago.

The Jewish historian Josephus provides a graphic and chilling account of the horrors and suffering of that time. (Whiston 1960)

Again, Jesus was not talking about a **global** event. His warning is directed explicitly to Jews still living in **Judea** in 69 AD. (Matt. 24:16).

Of course, Christians throughout history have experienced times of tribulation. Jesus tells us: *In the world you will have trouble (tribulation). But take heart! I have overcome the world.* (Jn.16: 33)

We in America have been most fortunate. Saints in some other lands have been less fortunate. Believers are still laying down their lives for the Gospel. Revelation has a word of comfort for all who are going through tribulation.

John saw a multitude *from every nation, tribe, people, and language.* They are wearing white robes, waving palm branches, and worshipping God on the throne. John was told:

*These are they who have come out of **great tribulation**; they have washed their robes and made them white in the blood of the Lamb.* (Rev.8:14).

We will meet these victorious saints again at the opening of the sixth seal in my chapter on **The Lamb and the Throne**.

HEAVENLY BODIES SHAKEN

Jesus continued his discourse from the Mount of Olives:

But in those days, following that distress: the sun will be darkened,
and the moon will not give its light; the stars will fall from the sky,
and the heavenly bodies will be shaken. (Mark.13:24)

Jesus' poetic imagery comes from Isaiah's prophecy against Babylon. (Isa. 3) The sun and moon are darkened by the smoke of burning cities. This imagery is used extensively in Ezekiel, and in Revelation. The stars falling from the sky may refer to the downfall of great kings and important religious leaders.

Jesus was using Isaiah's imagery for Jerusalem and the temple. The destruction once prophesied for Babylon was now directed toward Jerusalem.

The falling stars may be a reference to the priestly form of Judaism, with its animal sacrifices and temple worship. That came to an end with the destruction of the temple in 70 AD.[2]

That branch of Judaism had failed to produce fruit and was cut off. But God had not forsaken the Jewish people. Another branch, the Pharisees, survived as Rabbinical Judaism, and has continued to bear fruit to this day.[3]

There is one more part to Jesus' discourse from the Mount of Olives. We will take up this part in our final chapter, **Coming In Clouds**. But for now, it is time to introduce the book of Revelation, surely the most difficult and controversial book in the New Testament.

CHAPTER 7

Apocalypse
A message of hope when the going gets tough.

The revelation of Jesus Christ, which God gave him to show his servants what must soon take place. (Rev. 1:1)

The Apocalypse! In popular culture, it spells "Doomsday," "the End of Time," and "The End of the World." Movies and books spell "Apocalypse" in fiery letters against a background of exploding buildings and planetary catastrophe.

But apocalypse is not a doomsday word. It is a Greek word meaning "to reveal," "the unveiling," or "revelation." The book of Revelation is the unveiling of the risen Christ.

In scripture, apocalypse usually has a good connotation. Simon describes baby Jesus as a *light for* **revelation** *to the Gentiles and for glory to your people Israel.* (Luke 2:32). In the apostle Paul's epistles, we find the word apocalypse used as highlighted in the following passages:

*The mystery of Christ which was not made known to men in other generations as it has now been **revealed** by the Spirit to God's holy apostles and prophets.* (Eph. 3:5)

No eye has seen, no ear has heard, no mind has conceived what God has prepared for those who love *him - but God has **revealed** it to us by the Spirit.* (1 Cor. 2:9,10)

*God was pleased to **reveal** his Son in me so that I might preach him among the Gentiles.* (Gal. 1:18)

*The creation waits in eager expectation for the sons of God to be **revealed**.* (Rom. 8: 18,19)

This word apocalypse is also used twice for God's judgment of the wicked:

*...the day of God's wrath, when his righteous judgment will be **revealed**."* (Rom. 2:5)

*This will happen when the Lord Jesus is **revealed** in blazing fire with his powerful angels.* (2 Thess. 1:7)

The book of Revelation incorporates all of these meanings.

HOW SOON IS SOON?

The first verse in Revelation tells us it is about *what must **soon** take place*. In the final chapter, Jesus tells us, *Behold, I am coming soon...the time is **near**... Yes, I am coming **soon**.* (Rev 22:7,10,20)

What would "soon" be to John and his readers? A few weeks? Years? Centuries? How far into the future can we stretch "soon" before the word loses all meaning to its author and readers? Surely 2000 years in the future can hardly be construed as "soon." Those who project Revelation into our future are not taking seriously enough what the book actually says. The book itself sets the time frame for us:

*Write, therefore, what you **have seen**, what **is now**, and what will take place **later**.*(Rev.1:19)

What you have seen. The book is about things that John had witnessed in his lifetime. The event that profoundly impacted both Jews and Christians was the Jewish-Roman war of 66-73 AD. This event fulfilled Jesus' prediction about the destruction of temple, as we discussed in chapter 6 of this book.

We should expect to see this event in some of John's visions in Revelation.

What is now. Revelation was written 90-95 AD, during the reign of the Roman emperor Domitian. John was in exile during this time on the Island of Patmos, off the coast of Turkey.

This was a time of extreme danger for the first century church, both externally, and internally. The external danger was represented by the emperor Domitian.

Since the time of Augustus Caesar, Roman emperors were deemed to be divine. Roman law required all subjects to acknowledge that divinity. The Jews, however, had won an exemption from this requirement. As long as Rome saw Christians as just another Jewish sect, Christians were included in the Jewish exemption.

But the events of 70 AD served to widen the gulf between Christianity and Judaism. Around 90 AD, Jewish followers of Jesus were excommunicated from Jewish synagogues. The original Jewish leadership of the church had passed away by this time, to be replaced mostly by non-Jewish Christians.

It became evident to the Roman authorities that Christianity was not a sect of Judaism. As non-Jews, Christians were expected to acknowledge the emperor's divinity. Most Christians refused to comply.

Domitian took this refusal as rebellion against Roman authority and a serious threat to the empire. He responded with a campaign of repression and torture against the church.

There were internal threats within the churches as well. Paul had warned the elders of the church in Ephesus:

I know that after I leave, savage wolves will come in among you and will not spare the flock. Even from your own number men will arise and distort the truth to draw away disciples after them. (Acts. 20:29,30)

Paul's concerns became a reality, as we can see from John's letters to the seven churches in Revelation. Revelation chapters 2 and 3, Jude and 2 Peter all speak of divisive leadership, faltering faith, and faulty teachings in those *last days*.

What will take place later. John's life was sandwiched between two Jewish tragedies. First, the destruction of the temple in 70 AD. Later, in 132-135 AD, a false messiah known as Bar Kochba would lead a second unsuccessful revolt against Rome.

This revolt would end with Jews banned from Jerusalem. Jerusalem became Aelia Capitolina, a pagan city with a huge temple of Jupiter at its center. Jews were forbidden to live there.

The Jewish Jesus movement soon vanished from the pages of history. The rupture between Judaism and Christianity would be complete. An ugly anti-Semitism would creep into the church, which would play out in centuries to come.

But the *day of the Lord* would come for the Roman empire, in 476 AD. This too, John would see in his visions.

HOW LONG, O LORD?

They called out in a loud voice, 'How long, Sovereign Lord, holy and true, until you judge and avenge our blood (Rev. 6:9)

The cry *How Long, O Lord*, has echoed down through the ages. In every age, saints in one country or another have suffered for their faith.

Throughout time, people have wondered: "Why does God tolerate the terrible things that happen to innocent people—brutal rulers, oppressive empires, the destruction of war, senseless violence, and cruel injustice?" We wonder, "Will there ever be peace and justice in this world?" Some lose their faith over such questions.

Revelation offers hope to those who are suffering for their faith. It gives an answer for justice delayed. It calls for perseverance in the face of powerful adversaries. It promises victory over the powers of darkness and the entrenched evils of this world. And it gives us a glimpse of our world redeemed, restored, and renewed in the fullness of Christ.

APOCALYPTIC SYMBOLISM

Revelation belongs to a type of literature known as "apocalyptic." This type of literature employs a different set of conventions from the Old Testament prophets and the rest of the New Testament.

Readers in John's time were familiar with "apocalyptic" writings. There were many Jewish and Christian apocalypses in circulation, written between 200 BC and 150 AD.

Apocalypses are protest literature. They are intended to encourage the faithful saints during times of oppression by a foreign occupier. To disguise the meaning from the foreign occupier, apocalypses are written in symbolism. Oppressive empires are pictured as savage beasts.

The symbols would have no meaning for the occupying ruler. But the intended readers would recognize the meaning, because the symbols are drawn from earlier Jewish history and literature.

The visions in Revelation are like mosaic pictures. The tiles used to make up the picture are verses from earlier scripture, or events in Israel's history that remind the reader of what is presently happening.

We can get the meaning by tracing the details back to its source in scripture. This is not always an easy task, and we will not be able to solve every puzzle. But we can get the main ideas of the book.

The most obvious sources of symbolism in Revelation are Daniel and Ezekiel, and then, Isaiah, Jeremiah, Zechariah, the Torah of Moses, and the Jewish New Year.

The Jewish New year sets the stage on which the drama of Revelation is played. The Jewish New Year is the beginning of ten "Days of Awe," concluding with Yom Kippur, the Day of Atonement. The books of heaven, the seven seals, and the seven trumpets are all symbols drawn from the Jewish New Year, as we will discuss in the next chapter.

John the Baptist? Dr J. Massygberde Ford argues that the visions in Revelation chapters 4-20 have their source in the movement founded by John the Baptist. She points out that only John the Baptist calls Jesus *the Lamb of God*. And only in Revelation do we find the theme of Jesus as the Lamb. (Ford 1975)

John the Baptist's movement did not end with John's execution by Herod. There were many converts to this movement among the Jewish community in Alexandria, Egypt. Missionaries from Alexandria founded John the Baptist groups in Ephesus and Corinth, as we read in Acts. (Acts 18,19;1 Cor.1)

Very likely, the community that produced Revelation, and the Gospel and Epistles of John was closely connected to these groups. The name "John" may be a pseudonym used by several writers writing on behalf of this community.

Numbers in revelation. Numbers are used symbolically, not literally, in Revelation.

- **Seven** signifies fullness or completion. God created the heavens and the earth in seven "days." The Lamb has seven eyes, signifying the fullness of the Spirit. The Beast has seven heads, perhaps representing all the world empires that culminated in the Roman empire.
- **Three and half** (days or years) symbolizes the duration of evil. This figure reflects back to a time of great peril and crisis for the Jewish people in Judea, when the evil king Antiochus tried to stamp out the Jewish faith, as discussed in chapters 5 and 6.

The three and half years it took to overcome this reign of evil became a symbol of evil times, during which the saints groan under the burden of oppressive regimes. In both Daniel and Revelation it also appears as 42 months, and 1290 days.

- **Ten days** signifies a period in which judgment is deferred giving people and nations time to repent. This will be discussed in the next chapter, **The Lamb and the Throne.**

How we understand Revelation depends on the place from which we view its visions. Remember, from Revelation 4 and on, John is seeing things from **heaven**'s perspective. He and we are told:

*Therefore rejoice, you **heavens** and you who dwell in them. But woe to the **earth** and the **sea**, because the devil has gone to you.* (Rev 12:12)

The heaven dwellers. These would include the *dead in Christ*. But we don't have to die first to become a heaven dweller. Paul reminds us:

God has raised us up with Christ and seated us with him in the heavenly realms in Christ Jesus... For you died, and your life is now hidden with Christ in God. (Eph. 2:5-6; Col. 3:2)

We too, if we are in Christ, are heaven-dwellers. From this vantage point, Revelation is no longer a doomsday book. It is a book of hope. It promises victory over the powers of darkness, and a share in the glories of God in Christ.

76

The earth dwellers. In Hebrew, *earth* sometimes refers to the dry land, rather than of the whole planet. The "land" in the Old Testament sometimes is short for the land of promise.

John may be referring here to Jews living in Judea at the beginning of the Jewish-Roman wars of 66 AD. Jesus pronounced *woes* to the people of Judea, as we read in Matthew's gospel. Those *woes* were fulfilled in the destruction of 70 AD. (Matt. 23)

Or, this can be extended to all who are *in Adam*, who are *of the earth, earthly.* (1 Cor.14:47) For the earth-dwellers, Revelation can be a scary book.

The sea. In ancient Judaism, the sea usually carries a negative connotation:

The wicked are like the tossing sea, which cannot rest, whose waves cast up mire and mud. (Isa. 57:20)

They are wild waves of the sea, foaming up their shame; wandering stars, for whom blackest darkness has been reserved forever. (Jude:13)

In Middle Eastern mythology, the sea represents chaos, and the dwelling place of the dragon. In Daniel, four beastly empires emerge from the sea as discussed in chapter 5.

For these sea dwellers, the future looks really, really dark. In Revelation, both the heavens and the earth get transformed in the end. There are *new heavens and new earth.* But not so for the *sea,* for we read, *There was no longer any sea.* The unrepentant wicked are finally removed from the redemption story, along with beasts and dragons. (Rev. 22:1)

APOCALYPTIC THEOLOGY

This style of literature has its own theological perspective. Some common features of apocalyptic literature include:

- **Dualism** In Revelation, it is Satan against the Lamb. Satan's minions on earth are portrayed as beast and false prophet. This is in contrast to the strict monotheism of the Hebrew prophets, who leave little role for Satan in their perspective.
- **Cosmic struggle**. The troubles on earth are seen as a reflection of a battle raging in the heavens between forces of good and forces of evil.
- **Angels** play a major role, both as messengers, and as combatants. Good angels are arrayed against bad angels .
- **The Messiah, the resurrection, and triumph** over evil are apocalyptic themes.

These ideas reflect Jewish contact with the Zoroastrian faith during the Persian period. The Jews did not accept the teachings of Zoroastrianism. But it stimulated Jewish thinking and provided a rich source of symbolism for Revelation and other apocalyptic writings.

This is but a brief introduction to Revelation. A complete commentary on Revelation is beyond the scope of this book. However, in the next two chapters I will discuss three symbols most meaningful to me.

They are:

- The Lamb and the Throne.
- The Books of Heaven.
- Armageddon.

For a more comprehensive study of Revelation, I recommend the three *Revelation* books listed in the bibliography.

CHAPTER 8

The Lamb and the Throne
The central mystery of God's judgment.

Then I saw in the right hand of him who sat on the throne a scroll with writing on both sides and sealed with seven seals.
And I saw a mighty angel proclaiming in a loud voice, "Who is worthy to break the seals and open the scroll?" But no one in heaven or on earth or under the earth could open the scroll or even look inside.
I wept and wept because no one was found who was worthy to open the scroll or look inside.
*Then I saw a **Lamb**, looking as if it had been slain, standing in the center of the **throne**, encircled by the four living creatures and the elders.* (Rev 5:1-6)

Now we come to the central mystery and message of Revelation. John sees the *Lamb standing in the center of the Throne.* The throne speaks of God the righteous judge. The lamb speaks of God's redemptive purpose in Christ.

The Lamb at the center of the Throne tells us that redemption is central to God's judgment. **God's judgment is not primarily for purposes of punishment**. It is primarily about **saving humanity from its self-destructive impulses!**

For God did not send his Son into the world to

condemn the world, but to save the world through Him. (John 3:17).

The Hebrew scriptures point us in this direction. The Hebrew word for "judge" (SHAFAT) can mean to render a verdict or settle a dispute. But it also means to "defend" or "deliver." In each of the following passages, the word "defend" is SHAFAT, and can be translated as "judge."

*He (the righteous king) will **defend** the afflicted among the people and save the children of the needy; he will crush the oppressor.* (Ps.72:4)

***Defend** the cause of the weak and fatherless; maintain the rights of the poor and oppressed. Rescue the weak and needy; deliver them from the hand of the wicked.* (Ps. 82:4)

***Defend** the cause of the fatherless, plead the cause of the widow.* (Isa. 1:17)

When Isaiah declares, *Defend the cause of the weak and fatherless,* he doesn't mean to punish the weak. He means to stand up for them, plead their cause in the court, and deliver them from the hand of the wicked.

But in order to deliver the poor and needy from the wicked, God has to deal with the wicked. That is where God's wrath enters the picture, and woe to the wicked when that happens.

God's judgment also has the element of chastisement. *Whom he loves he chastens.* In the history of Israel, that chastisement was sometimes very harsh. But God only did what was necessary to save Israel from herself. Nothing less would have done the job.

Human sin has the potential of destroying humanity and taking down the rest of God's creation as well. This problem is not limited to individual sins. There are collective evils, some of which we have not yet even recognized as sin. These have to be dealt with if humanity is to survive and grow into its full potential as sons and daughters of God.

We can see God's judgment at work in the history of civilization. As civilization has evolved, it reflects both the fallen nature of humanity and the enlightenment of God's Spirit. There are "weeds" to be weeded out; and "grain" to be gathered in and preserved. God's judgment is part of this process, which goes on age by age, and generation by generation, as we discussed in previous chapters.

But it is the Lamb, standing in the center of the throne, who has made all this possible. The Lamb did what no one else could do. He broke the seals and opened the books of heaven. The world has not been the same since; He gave us an open future.

THE BOOKS OF HEAVEN

Dreams and visions draw their symbolism from the subconscious mind. John's subconscious mind was full of images from Jewish sources. One of those sources was the series of events known to Jews as the "Days of Awe." These days begin with the Jewish New Year, in Hebrew, Rosh Hashanah.

Rosh Hashanah occurs on the first of Tishri, the seventh month of the Jewish calendar. In our calendar, this would be in mid-September.

In the Old Testament, this was a minor "new

moon" festival featuring the blowing of trumpets. After the Babylonian exile, this holiday evolved into Rosh Hashanah, the Jewish New Year.

After the 70 AD destruction of the temple, Rosh Hashanah became linked with the day of Judgment, the coming of the Messiah, the ingathering of the exiles, and the resurrection of the dead. Jewish Professor Hayyim Schauss tells us:

> In those days the belief was already popular that Rosh Hashanah marked the day on which mankind was judged in heaven and man's fate sealed.
>
> At any rate, a generation or two after the destruction of the second temple, Rosh Hashanah had all the outstanding characteristics associated with it today. The Shofar was blown in the synagogue and various interpretations had been read into custom. (Schauss 1938)

John's visions reflect this Jewish tradition, and draw from it much of its symbolism. In particular, the sealed book, the trumpets, and the day of judgment are all features of Rosh Hashanah, and John's Revelation.

To understand what these visions meant to John, we need to become familiar with their meaning in Judaism. Note, what I am describing next are **Jewish**, not Christian traditions.

Judgment day once a year. In Jewish tradition, Judgment Day comes around once a year. Each year, on Rosh Hashanah, the books of heaven are opened. Each person's fate for the coming year is determined, based on their deeds during the past year. This applies to non-Jews as well as Jews, and to nations as well as individuals. Rabbi Zevin tells us:

> In Tishrei, the Holy One, Blessed be He, judges all the world's inhabitants as to all that will happen to them until the next Tishrei. As for countries, on this day it shall be decided which is for the sword and which for peace, which for famine and which for plenty. And mankind on this day will be accounted for, to be designated for life or for death. (Zevin 1981)

According to the Talmud, the books of heaven consist of three volumes: (Winter 1973)

The Book of Life. The names of those who are altogether righteous are inscribed in this book. This book is sealed on Rosh Hashanah. *Let him who does right continue to do right; and let him who is holy continue being holy.* (Rev. 22:11)

This is a small book, since most people are still a work in progress. The Book of Life appears in chapters 13, 17, 20, and 21 of Revelation.

The Book of Those In-Between. This is the book for those who are neither all wicked or all righteous. This is most people, so it's a very thick book. Most of us are a mixture of good and bad, with God's grace helping us to cope with our sinful nature.

This book remains open for ten days, from Rosh Hashanah, to the Day of Atonement, Yom Kippur. For these ordinary people, the door of repentance remains open through this period.

The Book of Death. The names of those who are altogether wicked are inscribed in this book, and the book is sealed on Rosh Hashanah. Their judgment is final, and cannot be altered. This idea is picked up in Revelation chapters 13 and 22:

If anyone is to go into captivity, into captivity he will go. If anyone is to be killed with the sword, with the sword will he be killed. (Rev.13:10)

Let him who does wrong continue to do wrong; let him who is vile continue to be vile. (Rev. 22:11)

Revelation 13 is quoting from Jeremiah 15:2. Jeremiah had just been told that God had rejected Jerusalem and set it for judgment.

This Book of Death is a small book, because relatively few people are altogether wicked. Most people have some worthwhile qualities. Or, as my daughter likes to say, "If nothing else, they can at least serve as a bad example."

Ten Days of Repentance. The ten days between the Jewish New Year and the Day of Atonement are called "the Days of Repentance." Because the book is open, its judgments can still be modified by repentance.

Observant Jews have prayers of confession, called the Viduy, which guide them through this process. The confessions include every possible sin of commission, omission, and ignorance. But this repentance involves more than prayer. The observant Jew must also go to everyone he may have wronged, seek forgiveness, and make amends.

If God is satisfied with what we have done, our sins are forgiven and our judgment is amended accordingly. This happens on the tenth day, Yom Kippur, the Day of Atonement. The book is then sealed until next year's Rosh Hashanah.

Jewish New Year greeting cards often say:

"May you be inscribed and sealed for a good year." (Schauss 1938)

OPENING THE SEALED BOOK (Rev. 6-11)

John wept when he saw the sealed book. The sealed book contained the fate of humanity. The seals meant that this fate was now inevitable. The human family had taken the path of destruction, and no one was able to change its course.

As the Lamb opens the seals, we get glimpses of what that fate entails. First, we see the dreaded "Four Horsemen." The horses and their riders probably represent:

- **The white horse**: Wars of conquest. Think of Alexander the Great and Adolph Hitler.
- **The red horse**: Revolutions and uprisings. Like the Jewish revolts of 70 and 135 AD.
- **The black horse**: Economic depressions and famine are problems faced by millions throughout history.
- **The pale horse**: Plague and every other cause of mass death and destruction. No region of the world is immune from the ravages of the black and pale horsemen.

These four horsemen are not something new, invented just for the end time. They have been riding through the pages of history from the beginning of time, and are still riding. If not stopped, these four horsemen would continue their deadly ride until the earth becomes a smoking wasteland devoid of life.

But the Lamb has broken those seals. We still have wars, revolutions, famines, and plagues. But they are no longer inevitable. Ethnic strife can be overcome. Peace is possible. We can have a more just society. Dread diseases can be conquered. Christ the risen Lamb has shown us the way. It can happen. It will happen!

SOULS UNDER THE ALTAR

When he opened the fifth seal, I saw under the altar the souls of those who had been slain because of the word of God and the testimony they had maintained.

They cried out in a loud voice, "How long, holy and true, until you judge the inhabitants of the earth and avenge our blood." (Rev 6:9-10)

John realized that the powers of evil are not kindly disposed to people of faith. People who stand for God's truth are often viewed as dangerous troublemakers by the powers that be. Many of John's fellow believers had already died as martyrs for their testimony. He himself was in exile for his testimony of Christ.

The souls crying out from under the altar in heaven were given white robes (a symbol of righteousness) and told:

Wait a little longer until the number of their fellow servants and brothers were killed as they had been. (Rev 6:11)

How long must they wait, and why? The martyrs got an answer, but in apocalyptic code. The answer is found back in Revelation 2, in the letter to the church in Smyrna:

*I tell you, the devil will test you, and you will suffer persecution for **ten days**. Be faithful even to the point of death, and I will give you the crown of life.* (Rev.2:10)

Why the ten days? This could not be a literal *ten days* as we know them, for Roman persecution went on for another two centuries. The symbolism of the *ten days* is drawn from the "ten days of repentance," which begin with Rosh Hashanah and conclude with Yom Kippur, as I mentioned above.

The *ten days* tells us that the day of judgment is being postponed in order to give people an opportunity to repent. As we read in Peter's epistle:

The Lord is not slow in keeping his promise, as some understand slowness. He is patient with you, not wanting anyone to perish, but everyone to come to repentance. (2 Pet.3:9)

But delayed judgment means delayed deliverance for the saints. Many will die without seeing justice in their lifetime.

This calls for patient endurance on the part of the saints who obey God's commandments and remain faithful to Jesus. (Rev.13:10)

Then I heard a voice from heaven say, "Write: Blessed are the dead who die in the Lord from now on." "Yes," says the Spirit, "They will rest from their labor, for their deeds follow them." (Rev. 14:3,14)

Now we can put the ten days together with the other numbers to create a contrast between *our present sufferings* and the *glory that shall be revealed in us.* (Rom.8:8)

- The martyred saints cry out, **How long**? The heavens are silent, but only for **half an hour**.
- The saints suffer for **ten days**, but they reign with Christ a **thousand years**, during which Satan is bound.
- The Beast is allowed to prevail over the saints for **half a week**. But the Beast is destined for the Lake of Fire, while the saints reign for a **thousand years**. (And they don't stop reigning after the thousand years).

The good news for us is that the books of heaven are still open. History is not pre-determined. The future can be changed. The four horsemen can be unseated. The planet and its people can be saved.

THE SIXTH SEAL.

I watched as he opened the sixth seal. There was a great earthquake. The sun turned black, like sackcloth made of goat hair, the whole moon turned bloody red, and the stars in the sky fell to earth, as late figs drop from a fig tree when shaken by a strong wind. The sky receded like a scroll, rolling up, and every mountain and island was removed from its place. (Rev 6:12-14)

This poetic imagery of stars falling like ripened figs, a darkened sun and moon, the sky rolling up like a scroll, and earthquakes is used by Isaiah to depict the fall of empires, kingdoms, and the rulers of the earth. (Isa.13:10;24:20ff;34:4.)

These terrors are first felt by the rich and powerful, before spreading to every class of society.

Then the kings of the earth, the princes, the generals, the rich, the mighty, and every slave and every free man hid in caves and among the rocks of the mountains.

They called to the mountains and the rocks, 'Fall on us and hide us from the face of him that sits on the throne and the wrath of the Lamb.' For the great day of their wrath has come, and who can stand. (Rev 6:15-17)

But there is no hiding place in the rocks and hills.

The *wrath of the Lamb*? What a strange image. Can you hear the cry, "Mad lamb! Mad lamb!" Mothers scurry to bring their children inside. The dreaded Lamb is on the prowl. Sound ridiculous?

A lamb is hardly an image to strike fear in the human heart. The Lamb represents the redemptive work of Jesus Christ. Why run from the Lamb, the symbol of God's forgiveness and love?

Some people just can't grasp the truth that **God is love**, we are loved by God, and God freely forgives our sins. His grace makes us worthy of his fellowship.

Like Adam and Eve in the garden, non-believers run from the voice of God. They flee from the Lamb who leads from death to life, and find themselves fleeing from life into death.

Perhaps that is why *The apocalypse of Jesus Christ* is perceived by so many as an "End of the World Doomsday" book. They are unable to see God's work in history - sowing the good seed, gathering the wheat into the barn, judging the nations, and purging the world of *all that causes sin and all who do evil.* They can only see their world crashing down around them.

But those who follow the Lamb have no need to hide among the rocks and hills.

The sealing of the servants of God. Those who have the seal of God in their minds need not fear the judgments revealed Revelation. They have endured and persevered in the face of suffering, and death no longer has any power over them.

The seal of God for the believer is the Holy Spirit. It is God's gift of grace to all who believe:

*(Christ) anointed us, set his **seal** of ownership on us, and put his Spirit in our hearts as a deposit, guaranteeing what is to come.* (2 Cor.1:22).

*Having believed, you were marked in him with a **seal**, the promised Holy Spirit, who is a deposit guaranteeing our inheritance.* (Eph.1:13,14)

John sees two groups who are to be sealed. The first group, the 144,000, probably represent the Israel of God—the faithful saints of the Old Testament, along with the first century Jewish followers of Jesus who made up the early church. (The 12 tribes x the 12 apostles x 1000 = 144,000.)

The second group, we are told, are a *great multitude that no one could count, from every nation, tribe, people, and language.* They have persevered through times of great testing, and have *washed their robes and made them white in the blood of the Lamb.* These are those redeemed from the Gentile nations down through the ages.

The seventh seal. The books of heaven are now open, as we observe in Revelation 10:2, in Revelation 20:12, and again in Revelation 22:10. The opening of the seventh seal now introduces the seven trumpets. This too, is a feature of Rosh Hashanah.

The seven trumpets are warnings of judgment to come. After the trumpets come seven bowls full of God's wrath. But *God has not called us to wrath but to receive salvation through our Lord Jesus Christ.* So the wrath part is beyond the scope of this book. (1 Thess.5:9)

CHAPTER 9

Armageddon
We don't need to go there!

*Then they gathered the kings together to the place
that in Hebrew is called Armageddon.* (Rev 16:16)

"Armageddon" in Hebrew is actually, "Har Megiddo," or the "Hill of Megiddo." Megiddo was an ancient Canaanite city guarding a pass through the
Carmel mountains. Later, it became an Israelite
town.

It was a strategic location, as every army passing
between Asia and Egypt had to pass by Megiddo. As
a result, the city was destroyed and rebuilt at least
25 times in its long history. Solomon fortified the city
and located his chariot depot there.

Today, Megiddo is an archeological park with a
small museum. It covers about 14 acres of ground.
(Not quite enough room for all the armies of the
world). The remains of Solomon's chariot stalls can
still be seen. Thousands of tourists visit this site
every year.

So what is the significance of Har Megiddo in
Revelation? To find the meaning, we go back to 609
BC, and the story of Judah's godly King Josiah.

Josiah was only 8 years old when he ascended to
the throne, after his wicked father, Amon, was as-

sassinated by court officials. He came to the throne after a 57 year period of darkness under the reigns of Manasseh and Amon. We are told:

Manasseh king of Judah has...done more evil than the Amorites who preceded him, and has led Judah into sin with his idols... Manasseh also shed so much innocent blood that he filled Jerusalem from end to end. (2 Kings 21:11,16)

Because of the sins of Manasseh and Amon, God had pronounced judgment upon Judah:

I am going to bring such disaster upon Jerusalem and Judah that the ears of everyone who hears of it will tingle...I will forsake the remnant of my inheritance and hand them over to their enemies. (v 12-14)

But Josiah turned to God and rejected the evil ways of his father and grandfather. At age 12, he began to seek the Lord. At age 18, he launched a series of reforms intended to undo the evils perpetrated by his predecessors.

Josiah led one of the greatest religious revivals in the history of Judah. He sponsored the refurbishment of the temple, tore down pagan idols and altars, and restored Jerusalem as the worship center of the nation.

But in 609 BC, the godly king Josiah was faced with a new crisis. The Egyptian army, led by King Necho II, was in transit through Judah's territory, to fight a series of battles along the Euphrates River.

King Necho sent an urgent message to King Josiah:

What quarrel is there between you and me, O king of Judah? It is not you I am attacking at this time, but the house with whom I am at war. God has told me to hurry; so stop opposing God, who is with me, or he will destroy you. (2 Chron 35:21)

But Josiah failed to recognize that God was speaking to him through this Egyptian king. After all, Necho was an idolater. What would he know about God's will for Josiah? Josiah dismissed the warning.

In the battle that followed at Megiddo, Josiah was fatally wounded.

Josiah's death ended Judah's last hope of averting God's judgment. Without Josiah's leadership, the ruling class quickly returned to its sinful ways. Jeremiah recognized what the untimely, unnecessary death of Josiah meant for the future of Judah. He *composed laments for Josiah.*(2 Chron.35:25)

Josiah's sons were thrust into responsibilities they were not equipped to handle. They did not have their father's faith in God. Against Jeremiah's advice, they foolishly tried to play Egypt off against the Babylonians.

The end came in 586 BC, when the Babylonians destroyed Jerusalem and the temple, and carried the people of Judah into exile.

This is the story behind the symbolism of *Armageddon* in Revelation 16. Armageddon represents the deception, tragedy, and futility of all the wars that have been fought throughout history.

In Revelation, Armageddon represents Satanic deception at work, deceiving the nations into going to war against one another. But the real aim of these wars is to counter the redemptive work of Christ. John writes:

*Then I saw three evil spirits, like frogs; they came out of the mouth of the **dragon**, out of the mouth of the **beast**, and out of the mouth of the **false prophet**... they go out to the kings of the whole world, to gather them for the battle on the great day of God almighty...Then they gathered the kings together to the place that in Hebrew is called **Armageddon**.* (Rev. 16:13-16)

DRAGON, BEAST, AND FALSE PROPHET

The Dragon represents Satan in his role as Destroyer, spreading chaos, fear, hatred, and pitting nation against nation and kingdom against kingdom. He is revealed in Revelation as:

The Great Dragon—that ancient serpent called the devil, or Satan, who leads the whole world astray. (Rev. 12:9)

Satan, in Hebrew, means "adversary." His mission is to oppose and obstruct the work of God. As the **serpent**, Satan is the deceiver. **Devil** means "slanderer," or "false accuser." He is *the accuser of our brothers, who accuses them before our God day and night.* (Rev.12:10)

The Beast represents world empires, who dominate and oppress lesser nations in their drive for hegemony. Daniel depicts the superpowers of his time as a series of predatory beasts, rising from the churning waters of the sea, as we discussed in previous chapters.

Each of these beasts had its season in the sun as the dominant world superpower. It is then overthrown as the next superpower beast rises from the sea.

There is a lesson for us in this. No nation is allowed to continue for long as the world's sole superpower. Power attracts power, and beast attracts beast. There is always another superpower waiting in the wings for the current superpower to falter.

Much of history—ancient and modern—has to do with rival superpowers competing for dominance.

In Revelation, John combines all of the beasts of Daniel into a single beast, with seven heads and ten horns. He is depicting the Roman empire, who had absorbed many of the spiritual and cultural qualities of the empires that preceded it.

The seven heads may represent Daniel's four beasts, plus the preceding empires of Egypt and Assyria, and then Rome. The ten horns may represent the small kingdoms who were subjugated by the Babylonian empire. Jeremiah 46-49 offers a possible listing of these kingdoms.

The Roman empire is no more. But that same spirit of superpower hubris and ambition is still with us, tempting nations with pride and arrogance to overreach to their own destruction.

The false prophet represents "religion in the service of the State." In ancient times, kings hired prophets to promote their war plans and to incite the troops with prophesies of glorious victory, like the court prophets I mentioned in chapter 2.

The False Prophet's job is to convince people that "God is on our side," and the enemy is the "evil empire." This spirit is still alive and active in our world.

John may have had in mind the Roman-appointed High Priest and his party, seen again in his vision of the prostitute riding the beast, in Revelation 17.

All wars involve some degree of deception. The people must be convinced that there is no alternative to the use of force. They are told "They don't know any language but force." "The enemy is subhuman." "We are the good guys, fighting the 'evil empire'." Those who protest are dismissed as unpatriotic and naive.

Josiah was a godly man and a great king. He had a great vision for what God wanted to do in Judah. But he allowed himself to be drawn into an unnecessary war. His vision died with him.

This is the meaning of Armageddon. **Don't go there**! It's not what it seems!

CHAPTER 10

Coming in Clouds
What we can know, and not know.

At that time men will see the Son of Man coming in clouds with great power and glory. And he will send his angels and gather his elect from the four winds, from the ends of the earth to the ends of heaven. (Mk 13:26)

The disciples expected Jesus to return in their lifetime. Jesus had said: *I tell you the truth, this generation will certainly not pass away until all these things have happened.*

This saying served to reinforce what Jesus had said on earlier occasions. As he began his ministry he told Nathaniel:

I tell you the truth, you shall see heaven open, and the angels of God ascending and descending on the Son of Man. (John 1:51)

When he sent out the twelve on their first training mission, he instructed them:

*When you are persecuted in one place, flee to another. I tell you the truth, you will not finish going through the cities of Israel **before the Son of Man comes.*** (Matt. 10:23)

On another occasion, Jesus told his disciples:

*I tell you the truth, some who are standing here
will not taste of death before they see the* **kingdom of
God come with power.** (Mk 9:1;Matt.16:28;Luke 9 27)

He told the religious authorities in Jerusalem:

*I tell you the truth, all this will come upon this gen-
eration.* (Matt. 23:26)

No wonder the disciples expected Jesus to come
in their lifetime. The apostle Paul apparently believed
the same thing:

*We who are still alive, who are left till the coming
of the Lord...we will not all sleep, but we will be
changed - in a flash, in the twinkling of an eye, at the
last trumpet.* (1 Thess. 4:15;1Cor.15:51)

Peter urged his readers to *live holy and godly lives
as you look forward to the day of God and speed its
coming.* He expressed his anger at those scoffers who
were saying, *Where is this 'coming' he promised?* (2 Pet
3:3,11)

AFTER THE DESTRUCTION OF 70 AD

Matthew's gospel was probably written a decade
or two after the destruction of the temple. Very likely,
his readers included Jewish believers who had fled
Jerusalem just before it fell to the Romans in 70 AD.

They wondered why Christ had not returned in
70 AD. For Jesus himself had linked the *coming of
the Son of Man* with the destruction of the temple, as
we read in Mark 13, Matthew 24, and Luke 21.

Everything else Jesus had prophesied in his discourse from the Mount of Olives had been fulfilled. The apostles had testified before governors and kings. The gospel had been preached to the Gentiles. The residents of Jerusalem had suffered the distress of the Roman siege. The temple had been destroyed by the Romans.

All of this, including the *coming of the Son of Man,* was expected to happen within the disciple's generation.

Most of that generation had already passed away by the time Matthew wrote his gospel. What went wrong? Had they misunderstood Jesus' words? Have we?

Let's take Jesus' *Son of Man* saying back to its source. It is a quote from Daniel 7.

DANIEL AND THE SON OF MAN

Daniel 7 begins with a vision of four beasts emerging from the sea. We discussed this in the previous chapter. But in verse 7, Daniel's vision shifts heavenward:

As I looked, thrones were set in place, and the Ancient of Days took his seat. His clothing was as white as snow; the hair of his head was white like wool.

His throne was flaming with fire, and its wheels were all ablaze. A river of fire was flowing, coming out from before him. Thousands upon thousands attended him; then thousand times ten thousand stood before him. The court was seated, and the books of heaven were opened. (Dan 7:9-10)

This scene is similar to the throne scenes in Ezekiel 1 and 10 and Revelation 4. They were all, with Daniel, seeing the throne of heaven in apocalyptic imagery. Then Daniel sees:

*There was before me **one like a son of man, coming with the clouds** of heaven. He approached the Ancient of Days and was led into his presence.*

But remember, Daniel is seeing this vision from heaven's perspective. This *one like a Son of Man* is ascending to Heaven. He is coming into the presence of God on the throne, not down to the earth.

Daniel was not seeing a vision of Jesus' Second Coming. He was seeing a vision of the risen Christ **ascending** to the throne of God in heaven.

This is what Peter saw on the day of Pentecost. Filled with the spirit, he declared:

God has raised this Jesus to life, and we are all witnesses to this fact. Exalted to the right hand of God, he has received from the Father the promised Holy Spirit and has poured out what you now see and hear. (Acts 2:32,33)

Daniel's vision of the *one like a son of Man* before the throne continues:

He was given authority, glory, and sovereign power; all peoples, nations, and men of every language worshipped him. His dominion is an everlasting dominion that will not pass away, and his kingdom is one that will never be destroyed. (Dan 7:13,14)

Paul had the same insight, as he wrote to the Philippians:

Therefore God exalted him to the highest place and gave him a name that is above every name, that at the name of Jesus every knee should bow, in heaven and on earth and under the earth. (Phil. 2:8-10)

Daniel then received a further insight:

Then the sovereignty, power and greatness of the kingdoms under the whole heaven will be handed over to the saints, the people of the Most High. His kingdom shall be an everlasting kingdom, and all rulers will worship him and obey him. (Dan.7:27)

The authority vested in the *one like a son of Man* has now been invested in the *saints, the people of the Most High*. This is exactly what the risen Christ told his disciples:

All authority in heaven and earth has been given to me. Therefore go and make disciples of all nations. (Matt. 28:19)

Jesus' words proved to be true after all. His prophecy of the *coming of the Son of Man* was fulfilled within that generation. But it happened in a way not recognized by the disciples (or by generations of puzzled believers thereafter).

Pentecost brought a *coming of the Son of Man* in the person of the Holy Spirit. The destruction of the temple in 70 AD was a *coming of the Son of Man* in judgment. Jesus' prophecy was **fulfilled**, but not **exhausted**. As my Broadman commentary notes:

In a real sense the Son of Man came and comes in judgment in each crisis situation where man is compelled to choose his destiny, whether at Golgotha, at the destruction of Jerusalem, or otherwise. (Ashcroft 1972)

THE SIGN OF THE SON OF MAN.

At that time the sign of the Son of Man will appear in the sky, and all the nations of the earth will mourn. (Matt.24:30)
Look, he is coming with clouds, and every eye will see him, even those who pierced him; and all the peoples of the earth will mourn because of him. (Rev. 1:7)

Matthew's community was still looking for a sign. (We note that only Matthew's gospel refers to the *sign of the Son of Man.*) What was this sign that would appear in the sky? It would be different things to different people.

The believer's sign. On Pentecost Sunday, the Holy Spirit came upon the disciples in great power. The risen Christ had come to them in the person of the Holy Spirit. As Jesus had told his disciples:

Before long, the world will not see me anymore, but you will see me. Because I live, you also will live. On that day you will realize that I am in the Father, and you are in me, and I am in you. (John 14:16ff)

For the Spirit-filled apostles, this was the *sign of the Son of Man.* The Spirit which they received was their sign that the *Son of Man* had taken his place at the right hand of God in the heavens. No other sign was needed.

The High Priest's sign. High Priest and his party ignored the sign given to the Spirit-filled apostles. So

106

their *sign of the Son of Man* would take a different form.

They would see the smoke of the burning city of Jerusalem darkening the sun and moon. They would see the Roman legions pulling down the stones of the temple. It would be the last thing they saw, but it would be too late for them. This would be the *sign of the Son of Man* to the high priest and his cronies.

The mourning of the nations. *All the nations of the earth will mourn* is a quote from Zechariah 12:10. It recalls the death of Josiah at Megiddo, as we discussed in the previous chapter. All the other nations will have their time of mourning.

In John's gospel, it is applied to Jesus' crucifixion (John 19:37). But this quote in Zechariah also contains a redemptive promise.

I will pour out on the house of David and the inhabitants of Jerusalem a spirit of grace and supplication... On that day a fountain will be opened to the house of David and the inhabitants of Jerusalem, to cleanse them from sin and impurity. (Zech. 12:10; 13:1)

That fountain was opened at the cross, and that Spirit was poured out in Jerusalem on the day of Pentecost. That same fountain and Spirit of grace is now open to all the nations of the earth. In the end, the result will be:

All nations will come and worship before you, for your righteous acts have been revealed. (Rev 15:4)

WHAT WE CAN KNOW, AND NOT KNOW

Jesus told his disciples on the Mount of Olives:

107

No one knows about that day or hour, not even the angels in heaven, nor the Son, but only the Father. (Mark 13:32)

Just before Jesus ascended to heaven, his disciples asked him, *Lord, are you at this time going to restore the kingdom to Israel?* Jesus answered: *It is not for you to know the times or dates the Father has set by his own authority.* (Acts 1:6,7).

There are some things we just cannot know. We cannot know with any certainty the details or outcome of the future. If we did, it would mean the future is fixed and unchangeable.

It would mean no "free will" decisions, for any such decision would result in a different future, one that we had not foreseen. The books of heaven would be sealed.

There are some certainties. We can be certain that God's steadfast love extends to all generations forever. We can be sure of God's salvation in Christ. We can be certain that God's redemptive purpose will triumph over all that destroys and causes sin.

CLOUDS OF UNKNOWING

*After he said this, he was taken up before their very eyes, and a **cloud hid him** from their sight.* (Acts 1:9)

The Son of Man is coming in *clouds of heaven.* He is still coming, and he is coming soon. His coming is not always what we expect. How is He coming next and when?

108

That is hidden from us in the *clouds of heaven,* the same clouds that hid the ascending Christ from the eyes of the watching disciples. For the *clouds of heaven* are clouds of unknowing. Paul wrote the Thessalonians:

We who are left will be caught up together with them (the dead in Christ) **in the clouds** *to meet the Lord in the air.* (1 Thess.4:17).

What does this mean? What exactly happens to us when we die? What is the nature of the resurrection body? What is heaven and where? How and when will Christ return? What happens after we *meet the Lord in the air?*

For the present, the answers are hidden *in the clouds of heaven.* At best, we *see through a glass darkly.*

These future events must remain hidden from our view, known only to God the Father. And because of this, we have an open future. Our decisions do matter. And we have a reason for our hope.

There is hope for the faithful people of God, and for all of humanity. That hope runs through the messages of the prophets as they faced the end of their age. It resonates from the songs of saints and angels in Revelation. We may have some hard things to work through in our own "end time." But the message of hope endures.

The plans of the Lord stand firm forever, the purposes of his heart through all generations...for the Lord is good and his love endures forever. (Psalm 33:11: 100:5)

These words are trustworthy and true. (Rev. 22:6)

BIBLIOGRAPHY

Archer, Gleason L. Jr. *A Survey of Old Testament Introduction.* Chicago: Moody Press, 1974.

Ashcroft, Morris. "Revelation." In *The Broadman Bible Commentary, Vol. 12.* Nashville: Broadman Press, 1972.

Charles, R.F.H. *A Critical And Exegetical Commentary on The Revelation of St. John.* Edinburgh: T & T Clark, 1985.

Clouse, Robert G. *The Meaning of the Millennium-Four Views.* Downers Grove: InterVarsity Press, 1977.

Cohen, A. *Everyman's Talmud.* New York: Schocken Books, 1975.

DeMar, Gary. End Times Fiction. Nashville: Thomas Nelson, 2001.

Feinberg, Charles L. *The Minor Prophets.* Chicago: Moody Press, 1952.

Gregg, Steve, Ed. *Revelation Four Views—A Parallel Commentary.* Nashville: Thomas Nelson, 1997.

Massyngberde, J. Ford. *Revelation.* Garden City: Doubleday, 1975.

Schauss, Hayyim. *The Jewish Festivals.* New York: Schocken, 1938, p186, 156

Strauss, William and Neil Howe. *The Fourth Turning-An American Prophecy.* New York: Broadway Books, 1997.

Whiston, William, transl. *Josephus.* Grand Rapids: Kregel, 1960.

Winter, Naphtali, Ed. *The High Holy Days.*
Jerusalem: Keter Books, 1973.
Zevin, Rabbi Shlomo Yosef. *The Festivals of
Halachah.* Jerusalem: Hillel Press, 1981.

NOTES

[1] Old Testament dates are from Archer's *A Survey of Old Testament Introduction*, page 495. Dates may vary by a year or more from other sources due to different dating methods. (Archer 1974)

[2] It was not the Jewish people as a whole who wanted Jesus put to death. It was primarily the Sadducees—the party of the Roman-appointed High Priest—who felt threatened by Jesus' movement. Jesus had many supporters among the common people and even among some leading rabbis, such as Nicodemus and Joseph of Arimathea, as we read in John's gospel.

[3] I do not hold to the idea that the Church has replaced Israel as the people of God. I believe Israel and the Church are both sustained by the same "olive tree" represented by the faith of Abraham, and are both included in the people of God. God also has *other sheep who are not of this sheep pen.* God's love is inclusive, not exclusive. (Rom.11:17; John 10:16).

Printed in the United States
143998LV00002B/1/P

9 781432 735593